CliffsN

Shopping Online

Safely

By David A. Crowder and Rhonda Crowder

IN THIS BOOK

- Explore the world of online shopping
- Understand secure purchasing
- Participate in online auctions
- Track down bargains
- Reinforce what you learn with CliffsNotes Review
- Find more information about shopping online safely in CliffsNotes Resource Center and online at www.cliffsnotes.com

IDG Books Worldwide, Inc.

An International Data Group Company

Foster City, CA • Chicago, IL • Indianapolis, IN • New York, NY

About the Authors

David and Rhonda Crowder were selling hypertext systems back in the days when you had to explain what the word meant. They have been involved in the online community for over a decade. Their Web site designs include the award-winning LinkFinder www.linkfinder.com and NetWelcome www.netwelcome.com sites. They have authored or coauthored over a dozen books, including *Setting Up an Internet Site for Dummies*, CliffsNotes *Getting on the Internet*, CliffsNotes *Creating Web Pages with HTML*, and the bestselling *Teach Yourself the Internet*.

Publisher's Acknowledgments

Editorial

Senior Project Editor: Nicole Haims
Acquisitions Editor: Andy Cummings
Copy Editor: Jerelind Charles
Technical Editor: Marsha Collier

Production

Proofreader: York Production Services, Inc.
Indexer: York Production Services, Inc.
IDG Books Indianapolis Production Department

CliffsNotes Shopping Online Safely
Published by
IDG Books Worldwide, Inc.
An International Data Group Company
919 E. Hillsdale Blvd.
Suite 400
Foster City, CA 94404
www.idgbooks.com (IDG Books Worldwide Web site)
www.cliffsnotes.com (CliffsNotes Web site)

Library of Congress Catalog Card No.: 99-66699
ISBN: 0-7645-8524-6
Printed in the United States of America
10 9 8 7 6 5 4 3
10/ST/RR/ZZ/IN
Distributed in the United States by IDG Books Worldwide, Inc.
Distributed by CDG Books Canada Inc. for Canada; by Transworld Publishers Limited in the United Kingdom; by IDG Norge Books for Norway; by IDG Sweden Books for Sweden; by IDG Books Australia Publishing Corporation Pty. Ltd. for Australia and New Zealand; by TransQuest Publishers Pte Ltd. for Singapore, Malaysia, Thailand, Indonesia, and Hong Kong; by Gotop Information Inc. for Taiwan; by ICG Muse, Inc. for Japan; by Intersoft for South Africa; by Eyrolles for France; by International Thomson Publishing for Germany, Austria and Switzerland; by Distribuidora Cuspide for Argentina; by LR International for Brazil; by Galileo Libros for Chile; by Ediciones ZETA S.C.R. Ltda. for Peru; by WS Computer Publishing Corporation, Inc., for the Philippines; by Contemporanea de Ediciones for Venezuela; by Express Computer Distributors for the Caribbean and West Indies; by Micronesia Media Distributor, Inc. for Micronesia; by Chips Computadoras S.A. de C.V. for Mexico; by Editorial Norma de Panama S.A. for Panama; by American Bookshops for Finland.
For general information on IDG Books Worldwide's books in the U.S., please call our Consumer Customer Service department at **800-762-2974**. For reseller information, including discounts and premium sales, please call our Reseller Customer Service department at **800-434-3422**.
For information on where to purchase IDG Books Worldwide's books outside the U.S., please contact our International Sales department at 317-596-5530 or fax **317-596-5692**.
For consumer information on foreign language translations, please contact our Customer Service department at **1-800-434-3422**, fax **317-596-5692**, or e-mail rights@idgbooks.com.
For information on licensing foreign or domestic rights, please phone +1-650-655-3109.
For sales inquiries and special prices for bulk quantities, please contact our Sales department at 650-655-3200 or write to the address above.
For information on using IDG Books Worldwide's books in the classroom or for ordering examination copies, please contact our Educational Sales department at **800-434-2086** or fax **317-596-5499**.
For press review copies, author interviews, or other publicity information, please contact our Public Relations department at **650-655-3000** or fax **650-655-3299**.
For authorization to photocopy items for corporate, personal, or educational use, please contact Copyright Clearance Center, 222 Rosewood Drive, Danvers, MA 01923, or fax **978-750-4470**.

Table of Contents

INTRODUCTION

Shopping on the Internet is fast, easy, and fun. You can find just about anything in the world without ever leaving home. No more waiting in line for some surly clerk to do you the favor of ringing up your purchase. You can use this book to learn about conducting safe shopping transactions from your computer.

Why Do You Need This Book?

Can you answer yes to any of these questions?

- Do you need to learn about making safe purchases online?

- No time to read a 500-page book on the secrets of e-commerce?

- Do you need to protect yourself from credit card fraud?

- Do you want to know how online auctions work?

If so, then CliffsNotes *Shopping Online Safely* is for you!

How to Use This Book

You're the boss here. You get to decide how to use this book. You can read the book from cover to cover or look for the information you want and put it back on the shelf for later. Here are a few ways we recommend searching for your topic.

- Use the index in the back of the book to find information or look for topics in the book's table of contents.

- Flip through the book and look for headings about specific topics, or check the "In This Chapter" list at the beginning of each chapter.

■ Look for more information in the CliffsNotes Resource Center.

Also, we placed these icons in the text to help you find information fast:

If you see this icon, make a mental note — this is important info.

This icon points out helpful hints, secrets, or useful advice.

This icon alerts you to things that require special caution. Be careful.

Don't Miss Our Web Site

You may be new to shopping online, but this book helps you get up to speed. Make sure that our Web site at www.cliffsnotes.com is your first destination. Here's what you find there:

■ Interactive tools that are fun and informative.

■ Links to interesting Web sites.

■ Additional resources to help you continue your learning.

Register for *CliffsNotes Daily*, a free daily newsletter sent right to your e-mail inbox each business day. See you at www.cliffsnotes.com!

CHAPTER 1

FINDING COOL PRODUCTS TO BUY ONLINE

IN THIS CHAPTER

- Surfing the E-Malls
- Searching for Bricks-and-Mortar online
- Seeking unique online retailers
- Digging up collectibles

Why is there all this hoopla about e-commerce? As the Internet becomes more readily accessible to the average person, the opportunity to do business in this new virtual venue has grown. We're sure that you've noticed the tons of places to shop online. But how do you find the stores and items you want to buy? In this chapter, we show you how to use the power of online search engines to find just about anything you can think of buying online, from everyday items to unique and unusual merchandise.

Prowling the E-Malls

For shoppers, malls offer convenience, as well as plenty of stores to choose from. But the down side for consumers, as you probably know from your last shopping experience, is that some stores have great merchandise and some have lousy merchandise. When you shop online, you have to be discerning — even more discerning than you would be if you were shopping at the mall in your hometown — because you can't touch merchandise before you buy it. Still, online shopping Web sites have a great mix of a lot of different types of stores that you can wander through, letting your web browser be the store window.

And now e-malls and specialty e-malls are popping up. *E-Malls* are Web sites that provide links to a variety of different types of shops that are all in one place, therefore making the virtual shopping experience that much more convenient.

The growth of online commerce has produced a couple of interesting differences between the malls of the real world and the new e-malls:

■ The advent of the *specialty mall,* where several stores that all sell similar items have gathered together in one cyber location, has brought about a feeling of specialization to the online commerce community that doesn't exist in your local shopping center.

■ If you've seen one shopping mall, you've practically seen them all. The fact is most malls contain the same set of stores from location to location. But on the Web, stores such as JCPenney, Sears, The Foot Locker, Victoria's Secret, and Radio Shack, which all cluster together in the outside world, have chosen to maintain a separate Web presence.

Table 1-1 gives the URLs of some popular e-malls.

Table 1-1:   E-Mall Web Addresses

Mall	URL
Buy Directory	www.buydirectory.com
Cybermall2000	www.cybermall2000.com
Empire Mall	www.empiremall.com

Mall	URL
Horizons Interactive Mall	www.horizonsmall.com
iMALL	www.imall.com
InterMall America	www.intermallamerica.com
MarketSuite Mall	www.marketsuite.com/shop.shtml
ShopNow.com	www.shopnow.com **or** www.internetmall.com
Virtual Reality Mall	www.vr-mall.com

Finding Bricks-and-Mortar Online

E-malls are a handy and convenient way to find a bunch of shops in one place, just as their bricks-and-mortar equivalents are in the real world. But there are zillions of online stores that aren't in e-malls. In fact, many retailers go their own way on the World Wide Web because the cost of setting up a solo operation is remarkably low.

Most retailers have registered every likely alternative you can think to their company's name and trademark — so there's no way you *can't* find the correct site.

For instance, the URL for the JCPenney home page (shown in Figure 1-1) is www.jcpenney.com/jcp/default.asp But you can get to the site just the same if you type **www.jcpenney.com**. To find the Web site for Sears, Roebuck & Co. type the much simpler **www.sears.com**. Table 1-2 shows the correct (and shortened) Web addresses for some popular online stores.

Starting Your Search Engine

If you're interested in something, you're not the only one. No matter how obscure you think a topic is, millions of other people on the Internet share your particular obsession. Whether you're looking for information about a type of product or looking for reputable online vendors, you have a variety of search sites, links, rings, and newsgroups that can help you narrow down your search.

Figure 1-1: The JCPenneys Web site.

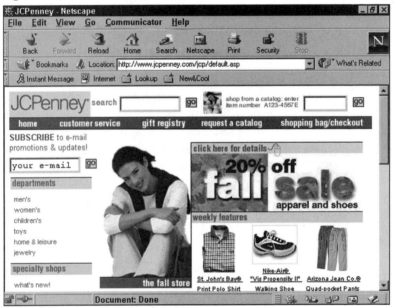

The biggest benefit of using these online resources is that a lot of the footwork is done for you. All you have to know is how to get to the information.

Tip

Often, you can use a combination approach to good effect by using search engines to find links pages, Web rings, and so forth on a particular subject. Try adding keywords such as **links**, **Web ring**, or **favorite sites** to your search.

Table 1-2:   Online Stores and Their URLs

Store	URL
Athlete's Foot	www.theathletesfoot.com
Babbages	www.babbages.com
Benetton	www.benetton.com
Beyond	www.beyond.com
Electronics Boutique	www.electronicsboutique.com
Footlocker	www.footlocker.com
JCPenney	www.jcpenney.com
Kmart	www.kmart.com
Limited Express	www.express.style.com
Lord and Taylor	www.maycompany.com/ Stores/lt_contact.html
Macy's	www.macys.com
Museum Shop	www.museumshop.com
Radio Shack	www.radioshack.com
Sam Goody	www.samgoody.com
Sears, Roebuck & Co.	www.sears.com
Sharper Image	www.sharperimage.com
Victoria's Secret	www.victoriassecret.com
Wicks'nSticks	www.wicksnsticks.com

Working the search sites

One of the best and most popular ways to find information about a particular item on the World Wide Web is to use search sites. These sites have huge search engines that can find just about anything you need. For example, the Yahoo! search site works by offering you a set of links to different categories and subcategories until you find your exact topic. Another search site, Excite, generates a set of links on the fly whenever you perform a search.

Both sites provide you easy searches that work essentially the same:

1. Enter your search terms, called *keywords*, in the text box (see using Boolean operators, in this chapter).

2. Click a button or press your Enter key to activate the search.

Figure 1-2 shows a typical search form.

Figure 1-2: A typical search form.

Using Boolean operators

Give a little bit of thought to the keywords that you use in your search before you get started because if your choices are too general, you'll get back a *few zillion* links and a *few billion* of those won't have anything to do with what you're looking for. The more specific you are, the more likely you are to get the results that you really want.

Most search engines also allow you to use *Boolean operators* to limit your searches. Don't let the terminology throw you. A Boolean operator is just a fancy way to say three little words: AND, OR, NOT. Table 1-3 gives you the low-down on how these words work.

Table 1-3:   Boolean Operators

Boolean Operator	Result	Example
AND between two keywords	Both keywords must be present in the search results.	You have your heart set on strawberry preserves, so you type **strawberry AND preserves** as your search term and find links to Web sites that use both words.
OR between two keywords	Either one of the keywords must be present in the search results.	You want to vacation in either Arizona or California, but not both, so you enter **Arizona OR California**, and you end up with links to sites that mention one or the other.
NOT in front of a keyword	All Web pages that contain that keyword are excluded from the results of your search.	You want to avoid California like the plague so you enter **Arizona NOT** of your search results mention that state.

To search for an exact phrase, put your keywords inside quotation marks. Your quest for strawberry preserves is more exact if you type **"strawberry preserves"** instead of **strawberry AND preserves** because using quotation marks forces the search results to include only those Web pages that hold those two words in that exact order.

Table 1-4 gives the URLs of several Internet search sites.

Table 1-4:   Internet Search Sites

Web site	URL
Excite	www.excite.com
GoTo.com	www.goto.com
HotBot	www.hotbot.com
LinkFinder	www.linkfinder.com
SavvySearch	www.savvysearch.com
Snap	www.snap.com
Yahoo!	www.yahoo.com

Using Web rings

Web rings are groups of sites on the same topic, each of which has, at least in theory, information to offer that the others don't. Each site in the ring has a link to the other sites in it, and you can follow along the ring to get more and more information on a topic.

The fastest way to track down a Web ring on a particular topic is to use the search engine provided at the WebRing site (www.webring.org). This site manages roughly a zillion different rings, and the odds are pretty good that you'll find a worthwhile Web ring using this site as a resource.

Using newsgroups and mailing lists

Newsgroups and mailing lists are other good sources of information. Many newsgroups and mailing lists maintain a document called a *FAQ*, or Frequently Asked Questions list. Nearly every FAQ ever created contains at least some links to major Web sites on the topic, and many of the sites have exhaustive lists of links that have been carefully researched and lovingly maintained to keep them as up to date as possible. You can also find a lot of links in newsgroup or mailing list archives. Sometimes the archives have their own search engine, which you can use to rapidly skim through old messages; other times, you have to plod through messages manually.

Digging Up Rarities

Sure, you can go to the Web site of a popular retailer like Sears or JCPenney, but what if you're looking for an unusual, used, or collectible item?

If you're looking for really offbeat items, such as go-cart accessories, a bottle of honey mead, the fourth book to complete an out-of-print series you're hooked on, or maybe a genuine ship's bell, look no further than the Web.

Finding antiques and collectibles

There was a time when a thorough search for antiques meant taking a vacation and driving from town to town, stopping off at obscure little storefronts every day or so with a wish list in your hand and a wad of cash in your pocket. Now, you can scour the whole world for any old collectible you want without ever even bothering to put on your shoes.

Antique dealers were among the first people to realize the commercial potential of the World Wide Web, and sellers of collectibles, rarities, and other hard-to-find items weren't far behind the antique dealers. You can see a tremendous overlap among these retailers, with many a store handling Louis XIV furniture, Merry Mice porcelain figurines, and Star Wars movie posters. Many antiques are also sold via auction sites, which are probably second in popularity to Web surfers only to online travel arrangement services. See Chapter 7 for more information on auction sites. Figure 1-3 shows you a popular online vintage dealer called Vintage Prints. Table 1-5 gives the addresses of several antiques and collectibles sites.

Figure 1-3: The Vintage Prints Web site.

Table 1-5: Antiques and Collectibles Sites

Web site	URL
Circline	www.circline.com
Collect A Doll	www.collectadoll.com
Gerald Murphy Antiques, Ltd.	www.gmurphyantiques.com
Margaretville	www.antique-center.com

Web site	URL
Antique Center	
Pacific Products Gallery	www.pacprod.com
Robbins Nest	www.robbinsnest.com
Sandy's Antiques & Collectibles	www.collectsit.com
Web site	**URL**
Treasures in Time	www.a1.com/treasures
Village Antiques	home.rica.net/dhaines
Vintage Prints	www.vintageprints.com

Finding unusual and unique items

Cottage industries bloomed early in the Web's history, and now you can find hand-made *everything* online. Artists making miniature teddy bears, blacksmiths forging replicas of Renaissance swords, and all sorts of other people, who previously had a hard time reaching their target audiences, suddenly find that they can reach the whole world all at once.

While that's good news for independent craftspeople, it's even better news for us shoppers, because we can get just about anything we can imagine.

Table 1-6 shows the URLs of some Web sites that carry unusual products.

Table 1-6:   Unusual Product Sites

Web site	URL
Exotic Mall	www.exoticmall.com
Rocky Mountain Meadery	www.wic.net/meadery
Starfire Swords	www.lightlink.com/starfire

CHAPTER 2

GETTING THE SKINNY ON WHAT YOU'RE BUYING

If the Internet isn't the greatest single source of information ever created, it's the greatest single collection of separate sources of information. With access to so much information, you have no reason for getting stuck buying a "pig in a poke" after you make an online purchase.

This chapter shows you how to find out all you need to know about using online sources, such as magazine reviews and newsgroups, to obtain information about a product before you buy.

Comparing at the Store

You comparison shop all the time. After all, few stores carry only one brand of shirt or one kind of desk chair. You look at how similar items are made and check prices for similar items before you make your final decision.

You may think comparison shopping is different if you shop online, but comparing items in an online store is just as easy as it is in the real world. If you comparison shop online, you should follow the same rules you follow when you shop in a retail store.

Compare products to:

■ Get a good idea of what most of the similar items have in common. If you find products that don't fit your criteria, you can quickly eliminate those items and concentrate on the ones that do.

■ Determine the minimum standard of quality for which you're willing to pay. If you're looking for a program for your PC, you probably don't want to buy one that's three years old and works with a Macintosh format, no matter how inexpensive it is. Figure 2-1 shows you a list of similar items for sale.

Figure 2-1:   Compare several similar products before you make a purchase.

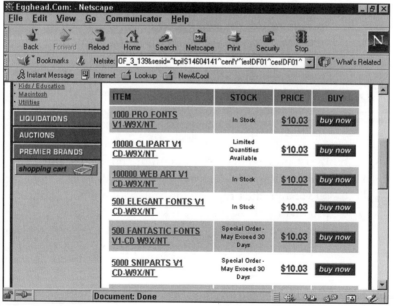

■ Find a product at a competitive price. If you find a program that meets all of your needs but costs more than the Hope Diamond, you may want to think twice before making the purchase.

Don't neglect offline sources of product information, either. Browse through your local retail store or a catalog to see if you can get a better deal or find a more enhanced version. And don't forget to ask your friends what they know about a product.

Going to the Source

The manufacturer of the product is a good source of information. Most manufacturers have their own Web sites, and sometimes their major distributors do, too. As with stores and most other outfits that have a presence on the World Wide Web, you can almost always find a manufacturer's Web site by typing the company's name (or commonly used acronym) into your web browser (see Chapter 1).

Most well-designed company Web sites set up links at the top of their home pages so that consumers can find more information on the company's most popular products (see Figure 2-2).

Every product has its limitations, no matter how well-designed it is. But no company that stands to gain from the sale of a product is going to spend a lot of effort listing the product's drawbacks. So, take a manufacturer's product description with a grain of salt, and don't accept a manufacturer's representation without comparing it with the opinions of others.

Figure 2-2:   A product image link.

Also:

- Look out for fabulous claims that aren't backed up. If a product is advertised by its maker as "the best in its class," you may think the product sounds great. Or you could do some research to find that many professionals in the field feel that no other program on the market is bad enough to be classed with that one.

- Note what the company *doesn't* say about its products. For example, if you're shopping for a new computer monitor and the computer manufacturer's site you've located doesn't mention screen resolution in its product description, you'd be well-advised to go out of your way to find out why before you go any further.

Finding Product Reviews

The main difference between company press releases and product reviews is that, although you may find either in a magazine, product reviews are written by individuals who don't work for the manufacturer. That usually means that the product has undergone at least some degree of testing. You get the benefits of the results in the review.

Thousands of Web sites have product reviews on them. Although reviews vary widely in editorial slant and content, most reviews fit into one of the categories in Table 2-1.

One way to find reviews for specific products quickly is to check a manufacturer's home page for review links. Of course, keep in mind that manufacturers usually provide links to those online magazines and testers who've given their merchandise good reviews or awards, but at least you've got a start.

Table 2-1:   Product Review Sites

Type of Site	Editorial Slant	Example
Test review	Sites that test a wide variety of products for consumers	*Consumer Reports* *Consumer Digest*
Specialized review	Sites that are dedicated to a particular topic	*Software Review Source* reviews only computer-related products
Online magazine review	Sites that review products that are only in their particular articles	*Stereo Review* magazine's review of a new sound system

Although most magazines are scrupulous about remaining editorially honest and would rather lose an advertiser any day than compromise journalistic integrity, disreputable reviewers *are* on the Web. Watch out for product reviews that only report on the glowing benefits of a product without ever bringing up any negative aspects, especially if the company that makes the product is a major advertiser in the magazine that published the review.

Figure 2-3 shows the *ConsumerREVIEW* Web site. This site provides mountains of information and does some of the fairest reviews we've ever seen. Table 2-2 gives the URLs of several Web sites that provide product reviews.

Figure 2-3:   The *ConsumerREVIEW* home page.

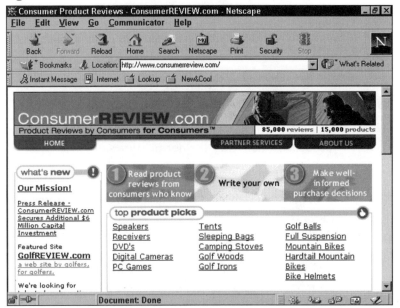

Table 2-2:   Product Review Sites

Magazine	URL
Active Buyer's Guide	www.activebuyersguide.com
Cadabra	www.cadabra.com
Consumer Reports online	www.consumerreports.org
ConsumerREVIEW	www.consumerreview.com

continued

Table 2-2:   Product Review Sites *(continued)*

Magazine	URL
Consumers Digest online	www.consumersdigest.com
Good Housekeeping Institute Buyer's Guides	www.homearts.com/gh/ toc/osinstit.htm
Stereo Review Magazine	www2.viaweb.com/mentormerc/ stereoreview.html
Software Review Source	www.reviewsource.com
WebShopper	www.webshopper.com

Working the Love and Grudge Sites

Some devoted people take the time to create Web sites about products, where they list horror stories or spread tales of products that just plain didn't do what they were supposed to do. A few also create Web sites that sing the praises of products that delivered on their promises. Of course, the "love the product" sites are not nearly as prevalent as the "holding a grudge" sites, (human nature being what it is), but you can learn a lot about the pros and cons of the products you're interested in and get a consumer's first-person perspective.

The great value to the consumer of these sites is that they reveal the real nature of the experience, showing you how a company can be supportive and helpful to its customers, or how it really doesn't live up to expectations.

To find the love and grudge Web sites, follow these steps:

1. Type the name of the product (or the manufacturer) that you're interested in into your favorite search engine's keyword search box.

2. To narrow your search down, add phrases such as **customer service**, **support**, and **problem** to your keywords.

3. Click the button (often called Search) to begin the search, and then look through and pick out the results that talk about actual experiences of real people. Check out Chapter 1 for more details on searching.

Talking to Other Consumers

The number one way to find out what you want to know about a product is to ask people who've had experience with it. While Web sites can provide a wealth of information, the sites may not be able to answer a specific question unless the question is common enough to be included in the site's list of FAQs. For meaningful interactive information about a product that you may want, you need to turn to live people for help.

Look for other consumers using the following resources:

■ **Newsgroups:** Discussion groups are conducted via news servers. Anyone can access a newsgroup because all newsgroups are circulated across the Internet, and most, if not all, ISPs carry them.

■ **Mailing lists:** Mailing lists are topical discussion groups that are conducted via e-mail to subscribed members.

■ **Chat rooms:** Online gathering places where several people can carry on a simultaneous discussion. Individuals type their comments, and all can read what others are typing

Each of these online resources is similar in that people use them to gather together and discuss subjects they're all interested in, but don't forget that you are dealing with strangers, so don't reveal personal information about yourself in any of

these venues. See Chapter 4 for more information about maintaining your privacy.

Don't forget that you can also talk to friends and family members who have purchased a product you're interested in.

Reading the newsgroups

Newsgroups are online text-based discussions on various topics. Tens of thousands of newsgroups exist, so you shouldn't have too much trouble finding one that covers any conceivable subject.

You must use a program called a *news reader* to both post messages and to read other users' postings, but the news reader is usually readily available from your ISP for free. If your ISP doesn't have a link to one, just drop in to www.download.com and take your pick from the latest news reader programs available. From the Home page, click the link labeled Internet, and then click the link labeled Newsreaders on the resulting page.

Deciding which newsgroup you want to subscribe to can be difficult because they don't come with descriptions. But newsgroup subscriptions are free and you can always unsubscribe if you're no longer interested.

Because you have so many newsgroups to search through, save time by using your news reader's find feature to search for keywords instead.

After you've subscribed to a newsgroup, you can look at *headers* to find out who posted a message, when the message showed up, and what the topic is. By just picking up this limited amount of information, you save time (and hard drive space). If you then see a message title that covers the subject you're interested in, then you can fetch the entire message and read it.

The vast majority of newsgroups are chaotic at best, and nobody's really in control.

Posting your own newsgroup message

If you don't find a newsgroup message that solves your problem, you can post your own message, which is sent out to every other news server on the Internet, and received by all of the newsgroup's subscribers. With luck, someone can help you with solid information.

Make sure that the title of your posting is easy to understand; news readers only display headers. Titles such as "Need help on..." or "Seeking info about..." let people who are browsing the a newsgroup's headers know right away that you want help.

Exploring mailing lists

Mailing lists, which tend to be better managed than newsgroups, are privately maintained. Most list owners go to a great deal of effort to keep out unwanted intrusions and distractions, such as unsolicited commercial messages.

You may find searching for a mailing list very easy if you go to one of the sites that is dedicated to categorizing and keeping track of them. Two such sites are:

- The *Publicly Available Mailing Lists.* (PAML), which allows you to perform keyword searches. Listings are located at www.neosoft.com/internet/paml.

- The Liszt Web site is another major (and user-friendly) mailing list listing, located at www.liszt.com.

The registration process for a mailing list varies just a bit depending upon the mailing list's software, but is something like the following:

1. Send an e-mail message to the listserver's address requesting that you be added to the group of subscribers. Be sure to specify which list you mean.

2. In the subject heading of your e-mail, type **subscribe list-name** or **join list-name** substituting the name of your chosen list for *list-name*. Sometimes, you need to specify your e-mail address, such as **subscribe list-name myaddress,** but most listserver software can get this information from the return address on your message.

3. Include the same text in the body of the e-mail.

You may receive an automated message from the listserver asking you to confirm that you wish to subscribe. The purpose of this message is to protect you from some malicious person adding your name to the list's subscribers without your permission. Reply to this message, following its instructions, and you're a subscriber. Ignore the message, and you won't hear from the listserver again.

If you want to send a message to other mailing list receivers, all you have to do is send an e-mail message to the list. Each of the subscribers receives your entire message because the list's software automatically distributes e-mail to all subscribers, including you.

The e-mail address of the listserver software is not the same thing as the e-mail address of the list itself. The former is used for administrative items such as subscribing or unsubscribing; the latter is used for sending messages to the other subscribers. Make sure not to send the wrong item to the wrong address.

Working the chat rooms

Chat rooms are virtual gathering places on the Internet, and they're even better than the newsgroups and mailing lists because you can often get your answer immediately. Unlike newsgroups and mailing lists, which require you to wait hours or even days before you hear a response, chat rooms are conducted in real time, and you have no waiting period for a response. The flip side of the coin, and the major drawback with chat rooms, is that you have to be in a chat room at the right time. That's basically a matter of plain luck, but you can increase your odds of success by trying chat rooms during prime time hours.

You use a chat program such as mIRC or Microsoft Chat to connect to a chat server. As soon as you're connected, you get a listing of "rooms" dedicated to various topics, much like the newsgroup listings in a news reader. From there, the process is simple: Find a room, sometimes called a *channel,* that covers the subject you're interested in; enter the room, and ask your question.

Normally, chat programs are divided into two portions:

■ An upper, larger, part of the screen shows what folks in the room are saying.

■ A lower, smaller, part of the screen is where you type your input.

After you press your Enter key, your input shows up on the upper screen, too. Everyone else in the room can see what you just typed and, with any luck, one of them knows the answer to your question.

If a chat room is particularly busy, you may find following the dozens of simultaneous conversations difficult at first, especially if you see a lot of letters strung together. You may be familiar with abbreviations such as LOL (laughing out loud) or TTYL (talk to you later) from using e-mail, but you may not know that these abbreviations originated in chat rooms. If you run across an abbreviation that you're not sure of, feel free to ask someone in the chat room.

Some Web sites also have built-in chat rooms that don't require chat software — they work right in your web browser. Check out Talk City at `www.talkcity.com` for an example.

CHAPTER 3

INVESTIGATING THE MERCHANT WITH WHOM YOU'RE DEALING

IN THIS CHAPTER

- Identifying online companies
- Checking the reputation of a business
- Conversing with the merchant
- Checking business references

Knowing who you're doing business with is often important, but if you're new to the Internet, how do you know who's who?

In this chapter, you can learn tips and tricks for making sure an online business is what it says it is. We explain how to use a company's domain name to identify the people in charge, clue you in on how to interpret trustmarks, and introduce you to a bunch of organizations that can keep you posted on what's going on in Internet fraud circles.

Identifying Companies

Except in the case of a big-name corporation, you're likely to start off pretty much in the dark about whom you're dealing with online. Sure, Sears is Sears, but who in the world is `aeiouandy.com`?

Using InterNIC's WhoIs service

InterNIC is the agency that registers Internet domain names and is run by a company called Network Solutions. A lot of information about any online company is available from this company, and its Web site's resources are free and open to the public.

To locate information about an Internet company through InterNIC, you need to use its WhoIs service. To do so, follow these simple steps:

1. Use your web browser to go to www.network solutions.com/cgi-bin/whois/whois. (See Figure 3-1.)

Figure 3-1: The InterNIC WhoIs page.

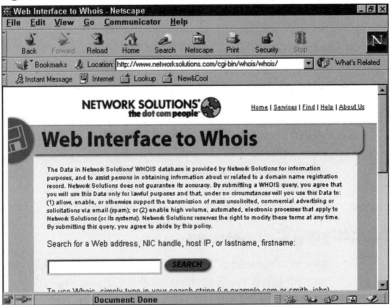

2. Type in the *domain name* of the company about which you want information. The domain name is the part of a Web address that identifies the company's exact location.

The domain name is just the tag end of the Web address, which means you don't enter the entire URL of a site when you're using the WhoIs service. For example, the CliffsNotes home page is `www.cliffsnotes.com`, but you only need to type **cliffsnotes.com** to find out more about the owner using WhoIs. Likewise, for information about the URL `www.linkfinder.com`, type **linkfinder.com**.

3. Click the Search button.

WhoIs digs through its database of domain names and returns the name and address of the company that registered that domain name, along with the names, telephone numbers, and e-mail addresses of various contact people for that Web site. The information may include the administrative contact, the technical contact, and the billing contact.

Accessing the WhoIs search system to search a domain name is the most popular way to research a site, but you have plenty of other access pages on thousands of other Web sites. A quick check through any of the major search engines turns up many more.

Using business directories

You can also find information about an online company using standard online business directories, which provide all kinds of data, from simple names and addresses to the latest financial reports, as shown in Figure 3-2. To be listed in an online business directory, a company probably fits one of the two following criteria:

■ The company is a real company with a Web presence, which is to say that the company started out as a traditional bricks-and-mortar-business and developed its Web presence later.

■ The company is a major Web company with huge Web presence.

Some online business directories charge a fee to use their research services.

Table 3-1 shows the URLs of several business directories on the World Wide Web.

Figure 3-2: The Fortune 500 offers financial information about companies in its database.

Table 3-1: Business Directories

Directory	URL
CIO Major Corporations	www.cio.com/central/businesses.html
Dun & Bradstreet	www.dnb.com/dnbhome.htm
Fortune 500	www.pathfinder.com/fortune/fortune500

Directory	URL
Hoover's Online	`www.hoovers.com`
SEC Edgar Database	`www.sec.gov/edgarhp.htm`
State University of New York	`www.sunysb.edu/library/company.htm`
Thomas Register	`www2.thomasregister.com/index.cgi`

Checking Reputations

Most small companies consider reputation to be nearly sacred. After all, reputation is a major tool when it comes to winning new customers. Because the overwhelming majority of commercial sites on the World Wide Web are small companies, reputation becomes even more critical.

Spotting phonies

Unethical or fraudulent companies are usually easy enough to spot right off the bat. Unethical companies most often are the ones that offer absolutely unbelievable deals. So, if a deal looks unbelievable, then it probably is. Likewise, if a company makes incredible claims about its products, watch out.

Here are some examples to tip you off that a company may be fraudulent:

■ Watch out for any company selling products that promise the seemingly impossible. For example, if a vendor is selling products that will make you lose weight without either diet or exercise, you may want to ask a few questions first. Ask a company that makes this type of claim to provide you with the results of its clinical trials and don't forget to check into any products' side effects.

■ Be wary of any company offering investment opportunities that will make you tons of money overnight, especially if the only requirement of you is *your* money. Make every company show you its proven track record and don't trust any company that only offers its most glowing predictions. After all, if the company is so incredible, how come you've never heard of it before? And why is it still looking for investors?

■ Beware of Multilevel marketing (MLM) plans, also known as pyramid schemes, which require you to regularly purchase products and then recruit other people to regularly purchase those products from you. Compare the prices of the product to those for similar products in stores.

Your best protection is your own common sense, so take anything you're told with a grain of salt. But you can also turn to several consumer protection organizations that keep track of companies' track records. You can also find a whole slew of Web sites dedicated to keeping you in the know about Internet scams and rip-offs. Internet Fraud Watch, shown in Figure 3-3, is just such a site.

Table 3-2 gives the URLs of other consumer protection sites.

Table 3-2: Consumer Protection Web Sites

Organization	URL
Consumer Project on Technology	www.cptech.org
Consumers Group	www.consumersgroup.com
Consumers International	www.oneworld.org/consumers
Cybercops	www.cybercops.org
Internet ScamBusters	www.scambusters.org
National Consumer Complaint Center	www.alexanderlaw.com/nccc/ cb-intro.html

Organization	URL
National Fraud Information Center Internet Fraud Watch	www.fraud.org/ifw.htm
PIRGs Fighting for Consumers	www.igc.apc.org/pirg/ consumer/index.htm

Figure 3-3:   Internet Fraud Watch.

Checking with business organizations

Unfortunately, you won't find an absolutely sure-fire way to check out the reputation of a company, because even if a company is a member of its local chamber of commerce and the Better Business Bureau, membership to these organizations is not necessarily a total guarantee of trustworthiness. However, belonging to such organizations is a general indication that the company isn't afraid of being in the limelight, and that the company has nothing to hide, which is certainly a step in the right direction.

The Internet has spawned widespread use of *trustmarks* on Web sites. Trustmarks are logos you find on Web sites that certify that the merchant complies with the standards of a particular organization, such as TRUSTe. You can click that logo to go to the organization's home page, where you can usually find information on the merchant, together with any complaints that have been filed with the organization against the merchant.

You should never weigh the significance of a Web site's display of trustmark over the entirety of your research. All of the little pieces create the whole picture.

The TRUSTe Web site, shown in Figure 3-4, adds its logo to online merchants who meet TRUSTe's criteria.

Don't read too much into the lack of a trustmark on a Web site. The absence of a trustmark signifies only that the merchant hasn't joined a particular group. Many merchants — the vast majority of them, in fact — are not members of any chamber of commerce or better business organization.

On the other hand, the presence of a logo is a plus, because a logo gives you some degree of assurance that the company isn't just a fly-by-night outfit that will take your money and run. After all, it does take a bit of trouble to get — at the very least, a company has to attract attention to itself from an organization that will scrutinize it — and most crooks won't want that to happen.

Table 3-3 gives the URLs of several better business organizations.

Figure 3-4: The TRUSTe site.

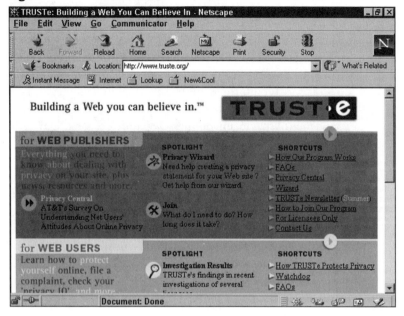

Table 3-3: Better Business Organizations/Trustmarks

Organization	URL
Better Business Bureau Online	www.bbbonline.org
BizRate.com	www.bizrate.com
CPA WebTrust	www.cpawebtrust.org
Cyber Commerce Commission	www.cybcom.org
Internet Business Bureau	www.inetbureau.com
SAFEBIZ	www.safebiz.com
TRUSTe	www.truste.org
WebAssured.com	www.webassured.com
WebWatchdog	www.webwatchdog.com

Talking to Merchants Directly

So far, every method we've recommended for finding out about a merchant has involved talking to other people or reading material written by other people. Often, the best way to get information on a merchant is to go straight to the source. After all, there are plenty of completely legitimate companies that aren't members of a chamber of commerce and aren't listed in any business directories, but are still worth dealing with, especially the small, mom 'n pop sites that are cropping up in vast numbers on the Internet.

If a company doesn't provide enough information about itself on its Web site to make you comfortable, one of the best approaches is to simply send an e-mail message to the company asking for more information about products and services that interest you. The section called "Finding Alternate Contact Information" in Chapter 1 explains how to locate e-mail addresses and phone numbers on a store's Web site.

If you can't find contact information for a merchant but the necessary forms for your payment are clear as day, you should think twice about dealing with the vendor.

Most small companies are more than happy to tell you all about themselves. In fact, if you're not careful, you're likely to get the life story of the owner thrown in for free. Ask for basic information such as:

- Where is the company located?

- How many years has the company been in business?

- Does the company operate only on the Internet?

- If the company is in a licensed industry, does it have a license number?

Of course, many companies on the Internet are brand new, or at least quite young, so you shouldn't necessarily disqualify a company if it hasn't been in business very long. Likewise, don't write an online merchant off just because it exists only in cyberspace. However, you're probably dealing with a much more solid and reliable company if it operates a bricks-and-mortar store or at least a standard mail order business in addition to having an online presence. And, generally speaking, the longer a company has been in business, the better the shopping experience you'll have with them.

If a company won't tell you where it is or can't give you a license number, then you're going out on a limb if you hand the company your money.

Checking References

Whenever you're about to make a major purchase, we think asking for references is a good idea. Of course, whenever you give others your references, you pick the folks you know will give the inquirer the best report. Beware. So do online companies. Still, asking for references is an acid test because if a company balks (or worse, can't come up with *any* references), that's a real red flag that there's a problem.

Call or e-mail the company's references and ask:

- How many times has the reference dealt with the company?

- How long has the reference been buying products from the company?

- Has the reference ever had any problems with the company's products, services, or delivery system?

- What did the company do to handle any problems that arose, and how does the reference rate the company's solution?

Newsgroups and mailing lists are just as good for telling you about the companies that make and sell products as they are for giving you basic information about products. See Chapter 2 for information on using these sources.

CHAPTER 4

HANDLING ONLINE SHOPPING ISSUES

IN THIS CHAPTER

- Understanding return policies and warranties
- Maintaining your privacy
- Dealing with spam
- Testing customer service

When you go shopping online, there are all sorts of aspects of a product that you have to consider besides the product's price. In this chapter, we give you hints on you making sure that you understand and agree with an online store's policies on returns and privacy. We also tip you off about restocking fees and extended warranties. You can also learn how to deal with unsolicited e-mail offers, otherwise known as *spam,* which invariably sound too good to be true.

Understanding Return Policies and Warranties

Sooner or later something you buy just isn't going to turn out to be what you wanted. So what happens if you need to return an item you've bought? Find out about return policies and warranties in this section

Reading return policies

When you visit a Web site that sells products, the company's return policy should be posted clearly on the site. You may find the policy in fine print at the bottom of every product page, or you may track it down to its own Web page after clicking on the appropriate link.

If you don't see a company's return policy, then make sure you send an e-mail message to the store asking what the policy is, and get an answer before you buy.

If a store has a no-return policy posted, then you can't dispute the purchase with your credit card company (see Chapter 9) unless the product is defective.

Paying for returns: Don't do it

If the store you're buying from charges a *restocking fee,* try to find somewhere else to buy. Restocking fees are a relatively new bit of nonsense meant to generate a secret profit for stores. Here's how the concept works: A company tries to charge you 15 percent or more of the product's purchase price, alleging that the company has to spend that much making an opened and returned product ready for resale.

Even in cases where a company really does take a loss on a return, this is a risk that all companies face as a regular part of doing business. There's no legitimate reason in the world to make the consumer pick up the tab for restocking fees.

Understanding warranties

Warranties vary widely, even among similar products. Some computer monitor manufacturers, for instance, offer warranties that cover three months, while others have warranties that cover three years. Because repairing an item after a warranty expires can be very expensive, we think you should go with a product that has a longer warranty — unless the difference in cost between similar products is tremendous.

A warranty isn't the same thing as a guarantee. *Guarantees* bind the manufacturer or seller to a promise, while warranties limit a manufacturer's liability if there's a problem with the item.

Most stores offer extended warranties, which can be either a terrible rip-off or a great benefit. To determine for yourself whether a warranty or extended warranty is worth your time, read the fine print and ask the following questions:

■ Does the fine print of the warranty indicate the people who built the product believe in it? If they think it's going to fall apart in 90 days, maybe you should think twice about buying their brand.

■ Does the extended warranty significantly increase the length of the original warranty? If you're only adding a few months to the warranty, you're not gaining much.

■ Can I get service more easily with the extended warranty? For instance, can you drop off the product at a local store instead of having to hunt up a warranty center?

■ Is the cost of the extended warranty so expensive that it isn't worth it? For example, if you're getting a modem for $80, and the extended warranty costs an additional $49.95, then you're paying too much.

If you pay for a product with a credit card, you may be able to skip buying an extended warranty. Many credit card companies provide free warranty services that double the length of the manufacturer's warranty, up to a maximum of one extra year. You don't have to pay for this service and you get the benefits automatically. The result is that if an original warranty is for 30 days and you pay with a participating credit card, then you receive a 60-day warranty. Check with your credit card company to see if your card has this benefit.

Maintaining Your Privacy

Many companies, both on and off the Internet, make some extra money — or sometimes their sole income — by gathering and selling personal information about consumers. Read on for information that can help you deal with online merchants that ask you to provide information when you fill out a form at a Web site, and check out Chapter 6 for more on privacy and secure Web sites.

Giving out information

If you're buying a product, the store has to ask you for some pertinent information — it's only natural. Acceptable information to give an online merchant consists of the following:

- Your name
- Your address
- Your credit card number

Sometimes, a company specifically requests that you fill out a special form for the purpose of providing demographic information on the company's customers. This is an entirely different matter than when an online merchant asks for private information as a requirement of completing an online order form (a big no-no), because divulging the information is strictly voluntary — you choose if you feel like sharing

Some online vendors add optional questions to online order forms in such a way that makes knowing whether or not you have to answer all of the questions to finish your purchase difficult. If you're asked for more than the necessary information in an online order form — personal information like your age, sex, and race — then an online company may be getting into things you shouldn't have to deal with just to buy a product.

If a purchasing form specifies that some information is required, while other information is not, then the required information is usually marked with an asterisk. Even when a vendor differentiates between required and optional information, though, the form doesn't always work right. If, despite the stated function of the form, you're actually forced to give out information you'd rather not, hit the Back button in your browser to back out of the deal.

Never say anything about yourself in an online venue that you wouldn't want the next stranger who passes you on the street to overhear. You should never divulge the following details when you participate in a chat room discussion, conduct an e-mail exchange, or fill out optional information on a Web site:

■ Password information

■ Real name

■ Financial background or account information

For more information about using chat rooms, newsgroups, and mailing lists, see Chapter 2.

Understanding privacy policies

Privacy policy statements are rapidly becoming a standard for companies on the World Wide Web. Privacy policies state things like:

■ What sort of information is gathered during your visit

■ How the data collected is used

Any time you visit a Web site, that site can get some information about you and your habits. All Web site software collects the same information about you, and while at first you may feel your privacy is being violated, don't worry, because all information is used to analyze the site itself, not to analyze you. Also, all the data collected about you goes into the Web server's log, which is held behind a *firewall,* or secure area. The most typical use of this information is to determine which pages on a Web site are the most popular. Information collected by most Web sites includes:

■ Which pages you visit

■ What image files you view

■ What site you just came from

■ What time you entered the site

■ What site you go to when you leave

■ What web browser (and version) you're using

Companies that show trustmarks (see Chapter 5) from organizations like TRUSTe have already promised to safeguard your privacy and not snoop into the details of your life. You can find several Web sites that specialize in providing information about online privacy. One site, EPIC, is shown in Figure 4-1.

Knowing about cookies

You may find it difficult to believe that files stored on your own computer can be personally invasive, but *cookies* can be just that. Cookies are files stored on your computer's hard drive that contain information generated by Web sites you've visited. While the normal Web server log information isn't linked to you, the cookies are, simply because they're on your computer, and not on someone else's.

Most cookies are harmless and even beneficial, enabling your computer to remember a password for a Web site so that you don't have to wrack your brain trying to remember it yourself. However, if you don't like cookies, you can prevent them from being created if you want to. Check out the Web site at `www.junkbusters.com/ht/en/cookies.html` for information on cookies and instructions on how to disable them in your web browser.

Figure 4-1:   The EPIC Web site.

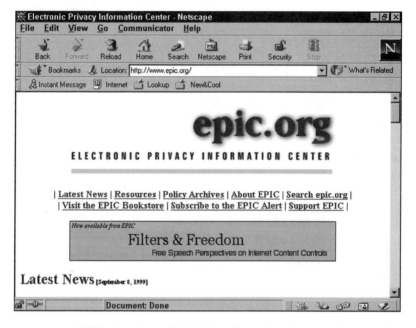

Table 4-1 shows the URLs of several Web sites that specialize in online privacy and cookies.

Table 4-1: Net Privacy Web sites

Web site	URL
André Bacard's Privacy Page	`www.andrebacard.com/ privacy.html`
The Dark Side	`www.cookiecentral.com/dsm.htm`
Electronic Privacy Information Center (EPIC)	`www.epic.org`
Online Privacy Alliance	`www.privacyalliance.org`

(continued)

Table 4-1:   Net Privacy Web sites (continued)

Web site	URL
The Privacy Now! Campaign	`www.eff.org/goldkey.html`
The Privacy Forum	`www.vortex.com/privacy.html`
The Privacy Page	`www.privacy.org`
Privacy Rights Clearinghouse (PRC)	`www.privacyrights.org`
Privacy Times E-zine	`www.privacytimes.com`
Your Right to Privacy	`www.rightoprivacy.com`

Dealing with Spam

From the day you get your first e-mail account, we guarantee that you'll receive unsolicited e-mail offers from lots of companies and individuals. *Unsolicited commercial e-mail* (UCE) is known colloquially as *spam*. Some of this junk mail contains legitimate offers, but most of it is garbage, plain and simple. We show you how to you recognize it and tell you what to do about it.

Understanding spam scams

Several tell-tale signs can clue you in to the fact that the offer in a particular piece of e-mail is a scam. The Federal Trade Commission lists 12 common ploys or angles to watch out for:

■ Promises of incredible business opportunities.

■ Bulk e-mail plans

■ Chain letters

■ Work at home plans

■ Health and diet products

■ Get rich quick schemes

- Free things

- Investment schemes

- Cable descramblers

- Guaranteed credit

- Credit repair

- Free vacations

While not all of these opportunities are necessarily fraudulent, they are the top dozen topics under scams. Some of them, like the cable descrambler, are illegal to buy and sell, regardless of how legitimate the offer may be.

There's also the possibility that some spam may have file attachments that carry viruses. The basic rule here is: don't open any e-mail attachments that come from someone you don't know.

Stopping spam

There are a number of programs available that filter your incoming e-mail messages based on either the sender's e-mail address or keywords in the subject line of the message. Several of these programs are available from the anti-spam Web sites in Table 4-2.

The easiest way to deal with unwanted messages, though, is to simply make liberal use of your Delete key. Just treat spam the same way you'd treat junk mail in your physical mailbox — toss it out. Table 4-2 gives the addresses of some Web sites that deal with the spam problem, and Figure 4-2 shows the CAUCE Web site, where you can report unsolicited email.

You can also report spam to the Federal Trade Commission (FTC), the governmental organization in charge of monitoring fraud on and off the Internet (see Chapter 9).

Table 4-2: Anti-spam Web sites

Web site	URL
alt.spam FAQ	www.ddi.digital.net/ ~gandalf/spamfaq.html
Anti-Spam Tools	www.newapps.com/appstopics/ Win_95_Anti-SPAM_Tools.html
Coalition Against Unsolicited Commercial Email (CAUCE)	www.cauce.org
Effective Action Against Spammers	www.windweaver.com/nospam.htm
Fight Spam on the Internet!	spam.fy-net.com
Netizen's Guide to Spam	com.primenet.com/spamking
Outrage Crusade Against Spam	www.dailyoutrage.com/crusade
Spam Tracking Page	www.rahul.net/falk
Stop Spam FAQ	www.just4u.com/webconsultants/ spamfaq.htm
Zero Junk Mail	www.zerojunkmail.com

Testing Customer Service

Before you buy a product, we think you should find out exactly how good the company's customer service actually is.

All you have to do to test an online company's service before you make a purchase is let your fingers do the walking. Make a note of the customer service phone number and give the company a buzz and ask a few questions. If you're thinking of putting a lot of money into a product, making a long distance call may even be worth your while.

Figure 4-2: The CAUCE Web site.

Ask customer service questions about:

- Prices (see Chapters 2 and 5)

- Delivery options (see Chapter 8)

- Response times (see Chapters 8 and 9)

- Technical support (see Chapter 3 and Chapter 9)

- Return policies (see information in this chapter as well as Chapter 9)

- Privacy policies. (see information in this chapter as well as Chapters 6 and 9)

- Specific, technical information about the product in which the company specializes (see Chapter 2)

Whatever product you buy, make sure that the company you purchase from knows more than you do about it. If you're buying embroidery floss, make sure the merchant knows its colors.

Have a hard copy of a company's posted policies on hand or have the merchant's Web site on-screen when you call so that you can compare the service representative's answers to what's posted online.

The cheaper alternative to phoning a company's customer service department, of course, is to use e-mail. Whichever approach you take, though, make sure that you ask enough tough questions that you can tell if a company knows what it's doing and can give you help if you need it.

CHAPTER 5

GETTING THE BEST DEAL POSSIBLE

IN THIS CHAPTER

- Exploring price comparison sites
- Haggling with a merchant
- Acquiring quantity discounts
- Searching for rebates and coupons

The biggest kick in any shopping expedition is making sure that you get the best deal you can. On the Internet, just as in the outside world, you can pay a lot more for the same item at one store than you would at another one.

In this chapter, you read how to find online price comparison sites, and we share a few tricks such as negotiating for a better price, using quantity or organization discounts, and taking advantage of manufacturer rebates and coupons.

Using Price Comparison Sites

Some stores go to incredible extremes to keep the prices they charge for their products secret. But the Internet is a place where free access to information is a hallowed old custom and as much a part of the Net culture as modem ownership is. So, it's not too surprising that the Internet has a lot of places where you can find out how much things are going for, and where you can get the best prices.

At price comparison sites you can do the following:

■ Browse through listings by product category.

■ Search for products by price and/or features.

Table 5-1 shows the URLs of several price comparison sites with one of these sites shown in Figure 5-1.

Table 5-1: Price Comparison Web Sites

Web Site	URL
Acses	www.acses.com
BottomDollar	www.bottomdollar.com
BuyCentral	www.buycentral.com
CompareNet	www. compare.net
Consumer World Price Check	www.consumerworld.org/ pages/price.htm
E-Compare	www.ecompare.com
PriceSCAN	www.pricescan.com
PriceTrac	www.pricetrac.com
PriceWatch	www.pricewatch.com

Haggling with a Merchant

If you're buying something from a bricks-and-mortar store, you're usually stuck with the price the store quotes. If a sales-person says a blouse is fifty bucks, then it's fifty bucks, and that's all there is to it. You can't walk in to a chain store and tell the person behind the counter that you think the store's prices are about 10 percent too high. Well, you can, but you won't get any results If you really like to haggle and get a good deal, read Chapter 7, which is filled with information on online auction and bartering sites.

Figure 5-1:   The BuyCentral Web site.

But the Internet is full of independent manufacturers, distributors, and stores. In a sense, the Internet is the greatest bazaar the world has ever seen. And if you enjoy the fine art of haggling, you can get even better bargains than the other online shoppers can.

Strategizing to haggle

You need to start out with the attitude that any price is only an *asking price,* a starting point, and realize that, for most merchants, any sale is better than no sale. Of course, merchants need to make a profit to stay in business, and you need to keep that in mind as you make offers. But also remember that any offers that are reasonably over the merchant's cost are profitable to the merchant.

Notice that we said *offers,* not *offer.* Making many offers is the heart of the haggle — the give and take, the testing of limits, the going back and forth between offer and counteroffer until you and the merchant find some middle ground where you can both be happy. Haggling adds a touch of fun to shopping for both you and the seller.

Sometimes, you can find the best price from one vendor but the best company to deal with in another. If you'd rather buy from the company that doesn't have the lowest price (but offers the best service), don't hesitate to tell the company that you can get the product cheaper elsewhere. If the company really offers better service, it may meet or beat the lower price.

Table 5-2 shows you how strategizing before you haggle with a vendor can save you money on your purchase.

Making an offer

When you prepare to make an offer, you need to have some idea of what you can get away with price-wise. Follow these simple rules:

■ Determine whether the item is a plain commodity or has some special value.

You may think that a scrap of leather with a few feathers fastened to it is only worth a bit of pocket change, yet we actually saw an item like this priced at $1,500.00. The reason? A famous designer's name was attached to it. Any item with *snob appeal* is probably beyond haggling over. But a *commodity,* on the other hand, is any product that has no particular distinction from another, similar product. Two brands of plain tee shirts, for example, have little to brag about between them, so make an offer.

■ Determine what the product costs the vendor. Most stores tend to mark items up to about double their cost, although there are a few exceptions to this general rule.

Table 5-2: Strategizing an Offer

Example Item	Vendor's Asking Price	Highest You're Willing to Pay	Your First Offer	Your Final Offer
Program that sells for $65 in computer stores	$59.99 plus shipping and handling	$65, including shipping and handling	$50, including shipping and handling	$65, including shipping and handling
Blouse that sells for $50 in clothing stores	$40 plus shipping and handling	$50, including shipping and handling	$45, including shipping and	$45, including shipping and handling
Car part that costs $250 and needs to be special ordered	$200 plus shipping and handling	$250, including shipping and handling	$200, including shipping and	$225, including shipping and handling

Most products, like software, books, compact discs, and computer equipment, which are in high demand, generate price wars that lower the profit margin tremendously. This means that you're probably not going to have much luck if you make an offer because the items are already being sold at close to their wholesale prices.

However, other items are much more profitable for their sellers. We saw a sprinkler with a retail price of $29.95 and a wholesale cost of 65¢. You can find out what the profit margin of an item is by simply calling the manufacturer and asking what the wholesale price is.

If you're dealing with collectibles such as coins, comic books, or antiques, check out the many price guides that are published. These guides show both wholesale and retail prices.

As soon as you have this information on your side, you're ready to haggle. Here's how it works:

1. Telephone the merchant and say that you're interested in buying an item, but you don't want to pay quite as much as the price the item is listed for. The merchant either asks what you had in mind or makes its own lower price offer.

2. State a lower price than you're willing to pay.

3. If the merchant agrees, take the offer. If the merchant doesn't agree, slowly nudge the price upward toward your real figure. When you both agree, and the deal is done.

Qualifying for Discounts

You may qualify for a variety of discounts both on and offline without even knowing it. To be sure, most online vendors aren't going to point out to you that you qualify, so you should know before you start shopping what kinds of discounts are universal. You can get

- Discounts for quantity.

- Senior citizen discounts.

- Discounts for being a student, teacher, or another profession, such as a hairdresser or a physician.

- Discounts for being a member of an organization such as the AARP or a chamber of commerce.

If you're going to be buying a lot of goods from a particular online vendor, you can often get a quantity discount. You'd be surprised how few items you have to buy to qualify for a discount. Normally, you think that getting any kind of discount takes buying hundreds of products, but many companies start their discounts with as few as five items. In most cases, you need to be purchasing several copies of the same item, but not always. Sometimes, sheer volume is the basis of the discount.

You may qualify for a discount if you're a member of an organization that has a deal with the merchant. To find out if any organization you're a part of has discount arrangements with any merchants, you can:

- Call up the organization's member services department and ask. If the organization doesn't have a discount plan, then urge the organization to provide this service.

- Go to the online search engines and run a search using the **organization's name** and **discount** as your keywords.

Using Rebates and Coupons

Sometimes you may come across a coupon or rebate offer for a purchase at a bricks-and-mortar store. Before you assume that you can use this offer in a purchase at the store's Web site, remember that depends on the fine print of the coupon or rebate, even if the physical and online stores are the same company. If you're planning on using a rebate or coupon, checking with the store before you buy is a good idea. Also, you can't return a product to a physical store if you buy it online, or vice versa.

We're hopeful that most stores with a presence in both the physical world and cyberspace will integrate their operations at some point so consumers can deal with either one interchangeably.

Finding rebates

Many real-world stores have manufacturer rebate coupons available, and the manufacturer of an item usually doesn't care if you buy the product online or not. Some bricks-and-mortar stores even have bulletin boards covered with hundreds of rebate coupons that you can browse through and snag at will.

In the online world, you can find rebates as well. For example, you can search for rebates on the Office Max Web site (see Figure 5-2). Office Max does rebates right — you can use the company's rebates on products you buy from the Web site as well from any on of its bricks-and-mortar locations.

Follow this process to find rebates:

1. Go to the Web site's home page.

2. Type a keyword that includes the word rebates. For example, on the Office Max Web site, the keyword is **maxrebates**.

3. Click the Search button.

4. A page appears, showing all current rebates. Office Max provides all available rebates for the current month, but the time frame varies from vendor to vendor.

5. Click the links to see the products in which you're interested.

Tip

If your keyword doesn't work, look for links that mention member perks. Some Websites have special pages devoted to perks like rebates, coupons, and discounts.

Figure 5-2: The Office Max Web site.

Generally, after you buy and receive a product, you need to go to back to the Web site from which you made the purchase and get the necessary instructions to receive your rebate. Follow these steps:

1. Go to the vendor's home page.

2. Look for a heading that mentions `Services` (as on the Office Max site) or `Member Perks` and click the link that refers to rebates (like the <u>MaxRebates</u> link on the Office Max site).

3. Another page appears, offering you several options. Click the link that refers to redeeming a rebate (for example, the <u>MaxRebates Redemption Form</u> link on the Office Max site).

4. Print out the redemption form and fill it out.

5. Scroll through the links listing various rebates and click the link that contains the number of your rebate offer.

6. Print out the tally sheet for your rebate offer and fill it out.

If you need help filling out rebate forms, you can always use a company's customer service number. Usually, you can find a list of customer service numbers on the company's Web page. If they're not listed there, just e-mail their Webmaster and ask what they are.

Of course, you need to follow all of the instructions and read the fine print when you fill out rebate paperwork. If you make sure to include all the information that you're asked for, such as the product's UPC code and a photocopy of your receipt, the rebate system works well. Don't forget to hang on to your original receipt, or if you must send the original, keep a copy for your records. Chapter 9 has more information on keeping records.

Getting coupons online

Besides using the Internet to make purchases online, you can get coupons online to use in the real world, which is the reverse of what you expect when you think of shopping online. Many Web sites have cleverly used electronic distribution in addition to placing ads in the newspaper and mass-mailing circulars to your home. The result is that you can gather coupons online for use in your offline shopping. You can find coupons for just about everything you can think of, from ice cream at Baskin Robbins to Red Baron pizza at your local grocery store.

One drawback to many online coupon sites is that they seem to be much more interested in gathering demographic data from their visitors than they are in getting you to the coupons quickly and easily. Some coupon distributors require you to register with the site before you can even get a look at what it has to offer. Registering with a typical Web site isn't usually a big deal because all you're asked for in many cases is your e-mail address and a password. However, some coupon sites require you to fill out some or all of the following information up front:

- Your zip code and county of residence
- Your age
- Your sex
- Your home address

You may say that filling out this information is a minor annoyance, especially if you need to give your mailing address anyway in order to receive coupons, but we personally prefer sites that make giving personal information an option, not a requirement. See Chapter 6 for more information on online privacy issues and choosing passwords.

We don't think coupon sites intend to be intrusive. For example, Coupon USA won't let customers browse unless they provide the site with their zip codes. But Coupon USA seems to be interested only in tracking where its visitors come from for demographics reasons. Coupon USA can also use the information to say to its vendors that a population of people from a particular area is interested in coupons, thereby increasing the variety of coupons for that population. If you decide to register to browse a coupon site, do the following:

1. Fill in the information asked of you or try to bypass the personal questions asked of you by clicking the Submit button at the bottom of the form without answering any questions. Some people even make up information to fill in the form.

2. After clicking the Submit button, narrow your search for coupons down to the state in which you're interested in (it doesn't have to be the state in which you live) and you then see the cities for which the site has coupons.

3. Click a city that interests you to see a set of links to the product categories for which the site has coupons.

4. Click a product category link that interests you to see individual coupon offers. Clicking a particular coupon lets you store the coupon in a shopping cart.

5. After you're done shopping, click the Print button on the Web page. A new Web page appears that contains the coupons you want.

6. Click the Print button in your web browser. The coupons then spit out of your own printer and they're just as good as the ones that you get in the Sunday newspaper.

Remember

The online coupon industry is still in its infancy, and you may have to do a bit of searching before you find anything you can actually use. Some coupon Web sites are so new that they have entire product categories that are just plain empty regardless of the location, and many of them, despite the global nature of the Internet, offer coupons that are for their own local regions only. However, the Internet changes very fast, and you have a pretty good bet that the selection and variety of coupons available online will grow rapidly.

The coupon industry veteran Val-Pak has a well-designed site that's as easy to use as its familiar snail mail coupons are, but don't be surprised if you find that most coupon sites leave you stuck clicking link after link and button after button before you find any useful coupons. Table 5-3 shows the URLs of several coupon Web sites.

Table 5-3: Online Coupon Sources

Web Site	URL
Clip and Print Coupons	www.grocery-coupons.com
coolsavings	www.coolsavings.com
Coupon Clipper	www.couponclipper.com
Coupon USA	www.coupon-usa.com
eclip	www.eclip.com
InstantCoupons	www.instantcoupons.com
Internet Coupon Directory	www.coupondirectory.com
Val-Pak	www.valpak.com
ValuPage	www.valupage.com
Web Kooponz	www.kooponz.com

CHAPTER 6

CLOSING THE DEAL SAFELY AND SECURELY

IN THIS CHAPTER

- Understanding secure servers
- Choosing payment methods
- Using secure e-mail
- Choosing passwords
- Making the purchase safely
- Utilizing offline payment methods

The first step in dealing with online security is to get over the fear of fraud (especially credit card fraud). Most of the horror stories that have circulated are just rumors and hype spread by people who haven't yet adjusted to the newness of e-commerce. The simple truth of the matter is that placing an order at a site on the World Wide Web is every bit as safe and secure as any other ordering method in the world. In the offline world, many store employees pay almost no attention to your security. Only in online stores do you find people who care about protecting you.

Credit card fraud isn't the only online security issue that you should be aware of when you make an online purchase. In this chapter, you can learn all you need to about ensuring that your online shopping experience isn't marred by a lack of security.

Understanding Internet Security

Every Web site uses a program called a *server* to exchange information with your browser when you visit the site. A *secure server* uses specially encoded messages to communicate with your web browser. These messages are *encrypted* (put into code) so that they cannot be read by anyone but the intended recipient.

You can easily see if a Web site is using a secure server. Look for:

■ Obvious indications on the site that security measures are in place, such as a message that announces the site's security, as shown in Figure 6-1. If you see no obvious sign of security measures, think twice before making a purchase. For information about trustmarks and associations that make a business out of ensuring Internet security, see Chapter 3.

■ A special secure server icon in your web browser. Both Netscape Navigator and Internet Explorer use a padlock icon to signify that you're using a secure Web connection. The Navigator lock icon is in the lower left-hand corner, and is also shown in Figure 6-1. The Internet Explorer padlock icon only appears if you're visiting a secure site.

Read and understand the privacy policy of any online vendor from which you're thinking about making a purchase. Check Chapter 4 for more information on privacy and security issues.

If you're just browsing a site and you're not exchanging information with anyone, security isn't a huge issue. But the second you begin supplying data to an online vendor or downloading data from the site you're visiting, you definitely do want to keep that communication strictly secure.

Not all Web sites use secure servers, and some sites that claim to be secure may not really be so safe, so know the security measures your browser uses, as well as how to find out if a site you're visiting uses security measures to protect consumers. See the following section for more information.

Figure 6-1:   A secure online order form. The Netscape Navigator closed lock icon is in the bottom left corner.

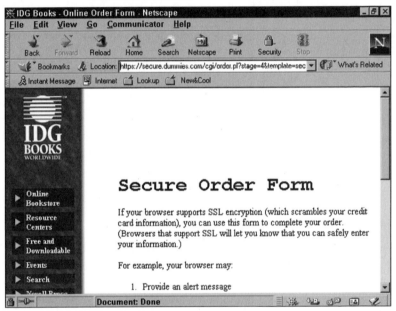

Letting Your Browser Work for You

You web browser's security system notifies you when you're about to compromise your safety. For example, many web browsers notify users with a dialog box every time they enter or leave a secure Web page. Also, most browsers warn you when you're about to send an insecure e-mail.

If you're filling out an online order form on what you think is a secure Web site and your a dialog box appears and warns you that you are about to send an e-mail to an unknown recipient, pay close attention. The dialog box, shown in Figure 6-2, is warning you of a pretty big security problem. If you submit the form, your personal information (your e-mail address, as well as the content of the form) could be intercepted, even if you don't *think* you're sending this information via e-mail. If you do get this warning message when you think you're conducting a safe transaction, we think you should abort the transaction. See the section in this chapter about sending secure e-mail.

Figure 6-2: Netscape Navigator's warning that you are about to send an e-mail to a potentially insecure site.

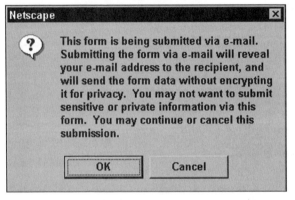

In a normal exchange between your browser and a secure Web server, if you fill out a form and submit it electronically, the information is encrypted so that it can't be read in transit. On a well-designed Web site, that information stays in a secure setting and cannot be accessed by anyone else.

However, some sites process form data using e-mail, which means that your security may be compromised because the form is leaving its secure setting and being transferred in e-mail to another location. This isn't a problem if you're not sending confidential information, but it totally violates the basic premise of a secure transaction. Pay close attention to your browser's warnings to you — you could be spared a lot of heart-ache if you do.

Choosing Safe Payment Methods

The most popular and safe method for making purchases on the World Wide Web is, just as in the offline world, is a credit card. Some companies, however, do offer alternatives, such as:

■ Debit cards, which work like credit cards, except that the payment is automatically deducted from your bank account instead of being billed to you later. Debit cards aren't quite as safe as credit cards, so watch out.

■ Checks, which you can either send through the postal service, or in some cases, send electronically. The electronic system works a lot like a debit card-transaction, allowing you to provide the merchant with the bank number, your checking account number, the check number, and the amount of the check. The online merchant creates an electronic debit of your checking account from that information. Paying by check doesn't give you many options for receiving a refund if there's a problem with the item, so use this option at your own risk.

■ Digital cash, which duplicates the features of paper money. Digital cash-systems typically require you to open an account at one of a limited number of banks that have signed on with the service, and then to use the necessary software to conduct the transaction. This software has to be run separately from your other Internet programs. Most digital cash-systems are modeled on the standard system of depositing and with-drawing money at your bank or through ATMs. Table 6-1 gives a listing of companies that deal in digital cash-systems and shows the URLs of their Home pages.

Under no circumstances should you pay for an item you buy online with cash because you can't trace cash and you won't get a refund. Checks are barely safer. See chapter 9 for details about troubleshooting completed transactions, and use a credit card.

Table 6-1:   Digital Cash Companies

Company	URL
CyberCash	www.cybercash.com
DigiCash	www.digicash.com
e-gold	www.e-gold.com
e-Money Systems	www.emoneysystems.com
InterCoin	www.intercoin.com
LETSystems	www.gmlets.u-net.com
Mondex Electronic Cash	www.mondex.com/ mec_noflash.html
The NetBill Project	www.ini.cmu.edu/netbill
NetCash	www.gost.isi.edu/ gost-group/products/netcash
WebCash	www.webcash.com

Digital cash systems are currently very complex and not anywhere near ready to compete with the simplicity and ease of credit card purchasing. Checks and debit cards don't offer you any protection if you have a problematic transaction and want your money back. See Chapter 9.

If you're not comfortable with the idea of sending your credit card information over the Internet, regardless of the safeguards, then you can always send the information offline. You have to go to a little bit of extra trouble, but if it makes you feel safer, then by all means do it. Just check the Web site for alternate contact information.

If you have no way to reach an online company other through its Web site you probably shouldn't be dealing with the company to begin with.

Using Secure E-Mail

Using e-mail to send credit card information is occasionally necessary. You won't find this situation cropping up very often, but it does happen from time to time. For instance, we had to order some photocopied documents from Great Britain, and the organization that had the originals was not a commercial Web operation, but an historical association. We could, of course, have used other approaches to send the information, but other methods would have been very slow and comparatively difficult. If you have no other choice but to use e-mail to complete a transaction, keep reading to find out how to reduce the risks.

Splitting data

E-mail can be intercepted and read as it passes from you to your intended recipient because e-mail gets sent along whatever electronic pathway happens to be available at the moment To reduce the risk of having your e-mail intercepted, split your data.

Whenever we need to e-mail personal information, such as a credit card number, we send half the credit card number in one message, half in another, and the expiration date in a third. The odds that one person can intercept all three messages, each going by a different random route, are astronomically low. Your Internet Service Provider and to the intended recipient of your e-mail are the only two sources who can see all three e-mails. Because you already trust both of these sources, the risk to your security is controlled.

Encrypting messages

Another option that's simpler than splitting data is *encryption*. When you encrypt your e-mail, you use special software to translate your message into a code that is very difficult to break. Breaking the code is not impossible, but it's also not worth the effort; doing so would require the assets of a major intelligence organization.

There are two problems with encrypting e-mail:

■ There is no accepted standard for e-mail encryption You have several different approaches to the problem, and you have to make sure that both you and the person you're sending the coded message to are using the same encryption software. Otherwise, the recipient will never be able to read your e-mail.

■ Both you and the recipient need to know the password in order to unlock the code, and the password has to be sent unencrypted. You need to let the recipients know about the password in some manner, or they can't read your message at all.

Remember

If you decide to use encryption software to send secure e-mail, you can send passwords via split e-mail, as described in the preceding section, through the postal service, or by phone or fax. But if you're going to go to all that trouble, you may as well just phone, mail, e-mail, or fax your order to the company while you're at it.

Unfortunately, encrypted e-mail isn't much of an answer for online shopping just yet — encryption is best used for business or personal matters until a standard emerges that's implemented in all the major e-mail programs.

Choosing Passwords

Many times, a Web sites offer an extra layer of security by only allowing you access if you enter a user name and a password into a dialog box (see Figure 6-3).

Here's a list of possible scenarios where you may need to use a password while shopping online:

■ Sometimes you need a password to access sites, such as sites that provide financial information for investors.

■ Sometimes you need a password to access some specific part of a site, such as a members-only forum.

■ Sometimes you need a password in order to get access to your own personal data.

Figure 6-3:   A typical password entry.

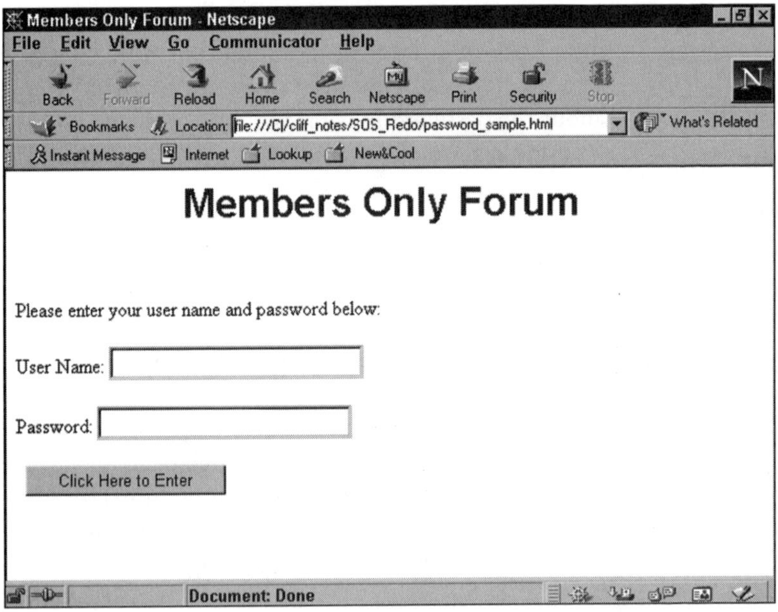

Remember

Rarely, a Web site assigns you a password, but most often, you have to pick one yourself, along with a user name. Passwords are usually restricted to a particular length, commonly between four to ten characters.

Here are a few guidelines to help you avoid picking a bad password:

- **Never use your own name as your password.** Your name is way too obvious, yet you'd be shocked at how many people do this. Or they'll use their middle name, the name of their girlfriend, children, or some other name that's just as easy for someone who knows them to guess.

- **Never pick a password that naturally follows from your user name.** For instance, if your user name is "ham," then don't pick "eggs" for your password.

- **Try to always use a mix of numbers and letters.** If you just use a plain word for your password, someone else can figure it out much easier. Adding some numbers adds greatly to the complexity of the password. Using the preceding example, you can actually be fairly safe by using "eggs4712" as your password.

- **Never use the same password twice.** If the security of one of your accounts is compromised, then all of your accounts that use that same password are endangered as well.

- **Always write your password down, even if you think you can remember it.** Even if the password seems easy to remember, you should still write it down. Keeping a couple of dozen passwords straight in your memory can be pretty hard, especially if some of them are for sites you don't visit regularly.

■ **Never leave your password lying around.** No matter how careful you are in picking a password, it isn't secure if you don't protect it. We're amazed by the number of times we've seen passwords taped to people's computer monitors.

Change your password from time to time. If you have a password for a Web site that is very important to you, change the password more often than usual.

Making the Purchase

When you're ready to make an online purchase, all you need to do is fill out an *online order form* to give the merchant your name, address, and credit card number. But before you fill out an online order form, be sure to read Chapter 4, which lists the information you should give a merchant, along with the information that's too personal to reveal.

Sometimes, if you have a wider selection of products to choose from, online vendors provide you with a *shopping cart.* Shopping carts are programs that emulate a physical shopping experience (as much as is possible on the World Wide Web) by letting you browse for awhile before you decide what you want to buy.

When you place an online order, keep a record of the transaction in case there's a dispute or problem down the road. If you place an order via fax, make a note of the fax number, the date, and the time, and keep your original document. If you mail in an online order form, make a photocopy of the form first. See Chapter 9 for more details on what you should save and why you should save it.

Filling out forms

Be sure to read an online order form very carefully before you fill it out, and be careful not to make a mistake. If a question on an online order form isn't clear to you, don't complete the form before you find out the answer to your question (searching the Web site's FAQ page or policies).

Online order forms contain many of the elements that appear all over the Web. For example:

- **Text boxes** allow you to enter information, such as your name or address. Forms are invariably composed mostly of text boxes.

- **Text areas** are larger than text boxes, and are typically used to provide detailed information, such as shipping instructions.

- **Check boxes** are used for selecting a non-exclusive option. For instance, if several different magazine subscriptions are offered, you can click on the check boxes for any or all of the magazines that you want.

- **Radio buttons** prevent you from giving conflicting instructions, such as ordering a large, medium shirt. When you choose between exclusive options, you're forced to pick one option, and you automatically exclude the others.

- **Drop-down lists** are list boxes that only take up one line because the options aren't visible until you click the list's downward pointing arrow. They are especially useful if the number of options is too large to fit on the form. Often, a list of each state in the U.S. appears as a drop-down list.

■ **Reset or Clear button** is used to erase all of the information you've entered and start from scratch. This button is most useful on a form with only a few elements. Why would you want to start at the beginning of a long form if you spelled your name wrong on the last line?

■ **Submit button** allows you to send in a completed online order form. Sometimes, the button says something such as `Place the Order Now`, but you'll know this button when you see it. Figure 6-4 shows a typical online order form.

Figure 6-4: An online order form with text boxes and drop-dead lists.

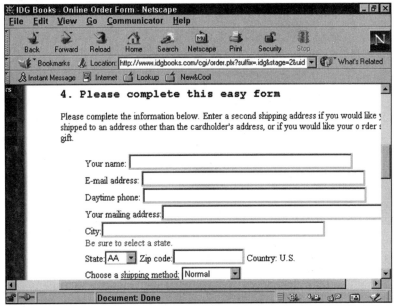

Using shopping carts

The only time you find shopping carts — or at least the only time it makes sense to use them — is if the store is so big that you have to look at several different Web pages to complete your shopping trip.

With carts, shopping is about as easy as it gets. All you do is click a button that says something like `Add this item to your shopping cart` and you can tote the item around with you as you shop. You can find these buttons on every page in the entire store.

At any time during your shopping experience, you can change your mind and remove an item from your shopping cart by clicking the button that says `Review the items in your shopping cart.` You're taken to a listing of all the items you added during your shopping trip. Figure 6-5 shows the product review page for a typical shopping cart.

Figure 6-5:   A shopping cart tells you how many items you're considering.

CHAPTER 7
BIDDING AND BARTERING

IN THIS CHAPTER

■ Finding online auctions

■ Placing your bid

■ Avoiding gotchas

■ Trading products and services

Online auction houses like eBay have become one of the hottest selling venues on the Internet. Every type of product you can even begin to imagine — including computers, antiques and collectibles, books, maps, and more — is up for bidding. In this chapter, we show you how online auctions work, and how to avoid getting into trouble over the rules of the house. We also look at alternatives to the traditional online sales or auction transaction. You can actually *barter,* or exchange services and products for merchandise.

What is an Online Auction?

You probably know how a real world auction works — the item's owner sets a starting bid and an auctioneer takes bids and sells the item to the highest bidder. The newest fad on the Internet is the *online auction,* which follows the principles of real-world auctions, and several sites provide auctions in some form or other. Check out Table 7-1 for a comparison of online auction venues.

In traditional online auctions, individuals pay a Web site a fee to set up auctions so that others may browse and bid on items. In many cases, the Web site takes no responsibility for authenticating items. Some online stores have begun to supplement their incomes with auction offerings. The seller in these auctions is the online merchant.

Table 7-1:   Online Auction Venues

Online Venue	Pros	Cons
Traditional online store	You know who you're dealing with and exactly what you're getting	You may be stuck paying more than you might elsewhere
Traditional online auction	You never have to pay more than you're willing to bid for an item	You have to trust the seller; no return policy
Mix between online store and online auction	Best of both worlds: You know who you're dealing with; Great deals; return policy	Worst of both worlds: The deals aren't always great

Finding Auction Sites

With so many sites that fit into both the traditional online store category, as well as the online auction category, you need to learn some techniques for tracking down sites that provide great auction deals. Two good approaches to finding the auction action online are:

■ Using a search engine, such as Yahoo! (See Chapter 1), type the keyword **auction** along with the search terms that apply to the item(s) you're seeking.

■ Check out the specialized auction information sites on the Web. These sites provide links to popular auction sites.

One of the best sources for information about online auctions is Auction Tribune, (See Figure 7-1) located at www.auctiontribune.com, an electronic magazine dedicated to providing solid information about online auctions. You find a tremendous amount of information if you're an online auction newcomer or a veteran. Table 7-2 gives the URLs of some of the best-known Internet auction Web sites.

Another good auction site is Auction Watchers. This site, which is devoted to computers and electronics, has an auction search engine that you can visit at www.auctionwatchers.com.

Figure 7-1: The Auction Tribune home page.

Table 7-2:   Online Auction Sites

Auction Site	URL
Auction Universe	`www.auctionuniverse.com`
Bargains on the Block (BOTB)	`www.botb.com`
eBay	`www.ebay.com`
ICollector	`www.auctions-on-line.com`
Live Auction Online	`www.liveauctiononline.com`
LiveBid	`www.LiveBid.com`
Onsale	`www.onsale.com`
Pottery Auction	`www.potteryauction.com`
SurplusAuction (Egghead)	`www.surplusauction.com`
uBid Online Auction	`www.ubid.com`
Utrade	`www.utrade.com`

Strategizing Your Bid

The heart of any auction is *bidding*— competing with other people to see who's willing to pay the most for a particular item that's on the auction block.

That's the funny thing about online auctions; the rest of online shopping is a hunt for a real bargain, but can be the exact opposite, depending on how much you're willing to spend, especially on an extremely popular or one of a kind item.

You find two kinds of items available for auction on the Internet, and each has its own type of bidding strategy:

■ *Commodity items* such as computers. With a commodity, you're shooting for a cheap price (cheaper than you would find at a bricks-and-mortar store or at another online retailer). When you find an item like this, strategize your high bid so that you don't spend more than you really want to.

■ *Rarities or collectibles.* To a real auction fiend, hunting for a rarity makes the thrill of bidding worthwhile. And when there's only one original *Star Wars* movie poster or a truly ancient Barbie doll in perfect condition, the competition can get pretty fierce (and the prices can go way out of sight). Know the market value of the item you want and cap your high bid so that you don't spend more than you can afford.

Always know who the seller is and what the terms of the deal are. Be careful when dealing with an auction site such as eBay, for example, which acts as a *venue* between interested parties. Venues don't act on your behalf if you're unhappy with a product, and most sellers don't have a customer service department.

Unlike auctions in the real world, which generally end after bids stop coming in, all online auctions have set closing times. If you're waiting until the last minute to enter a bid, make sure that you take the time zone of the auction into account — if you're in California and the auction's in Georgia, you may be three hours late when you think you're on time.

Placing a bid

Most auction sites don't force you to register until you place a bid. Follow the rules outlined in Chapter 4 about giving personal information online.

To place a bid in an online auction, follow this process, which of course varies from site to site:

1. Log on to the site.

2. If you're looking for a particular item, click the category link that is most likely to list that item. If you're browsing, click the links that catch your eye.

3. Choose the particular auction that you want to participate in.

4. Review the item or items available for bidding and pay close attention to the descriptions and terms of the sale. If the auction has several items available (such as 15 printers, each identical, manufactured by the same company), you don't have to bid on all 15 printers, but you can if you want to. Other auctions have only one item for sale.

5. If you like what you see, place a bid and specify the number of items you want if you have more than one to choose.

6. Enter your personal information, such as name and address, along with payment information (usually your credit card number).

Some online auction houses offer various electronic payment methods for bidding. While these methods may be safe, secure, and useful, they don't offer you the same legal protection you get as when you're paying with a credit card. (See Chapter 9 for more information.)

Using bidding extras

A lot of online auction houses go a little bit extra out of their way to assist you in participating. For instance, nearly every auction house is happy to keep you informed via e-mail whenever another bid tops yours. That way, you don't have to constantly keep an eye on the bidding to make sure that you're still on top, and if you really want to win, you have a better chance to do so if you're kept informed.

Some sites, such as Auction Universe and eBay, take that service one better — they have an automated tool that keeps you from having to constantly check in on the current bidding. The service, sometimes called a *proxy bidder,* automates the bidding process and is highlighted in Table 7-3.

You can set the *bidding increment* (the amount of money the software increases your bid until you reach your high bid) yourself on some auction sites. On other sites, the bidding increment is predetermined based on the item's current high bid.

Avoiding Gotchas

Online auctions have their own special problems that can crop up. Make sure you're familiar with the rules of a particular auction site before you place a bid to avoid being banned from an auction site and laying yourself open for both civil and criminal prosecution. All auction Web sites have rules and regulations posted.

In most auctions, sellers are independent users of the auction site. The deal you get on an item is only as good as the seller's word, so:

■ Make use of the seller's posted e-mail address and all questions you have *before you bid.*

■ If you can't contact the seller, then *don't bid* on the item.

If you're the high bidder, you win the auction, and that means you owe the seller money. This may seem obvious, but some people jump into the bidding as if it's a game. Don't act impulsively — in many states, a bid is a binding contract.

Table 7-3: Using a Proxy-Bid Service

Current Bid	Your Pre-Set High Bid	Bidder 2's High Bid	Bidder 3's High Bid	What the Bidding Software Does
$50	$75	$70	$80	Knocks Bidder 2 out after the bidding hits $70.
$71	$75	Knocked out	$80	Bids for you until bidding hits $75 and knocks you out.
$76	Knocked out	Knocked out	High Bidder	Bidder 3 is the high bidder. You can choose to set a new high bid, bid on your own, or give up.

Trading Products and Services

The *barter system,* which allows for goods to be exchanged for services (or visa versa) is probably the earliest method of exchange known to man; the system certainly existed long before anyone ever even thought of using money. Surprisingly, this "primitive" payment technique has found a strong niche in the ultra high-tech world of the Internet. Ideal situations for barter crop up if

- Your company and another company both have an overstock of products that the other wants. A computer store may trade some equipment to a car dealer in exchange for a van it needs.

- You're short on money, but long on talent. If you are handy with Web design and you're fond of French cooking, barter your Web design talents to a French restaurant in exchange for a few free dinners for two at *Chez Fancy Restaurant.*

The *International Reciprocal Trade Association,* or IRTA, is an industry organization that promotes the barter system. If you're interested in finding out how the process works, check out its Web site, shown in Figure 7-2 and check out Table 7-4 for the URLs of several other barter resources.

Figure 7-2:   The IRTA Web site.

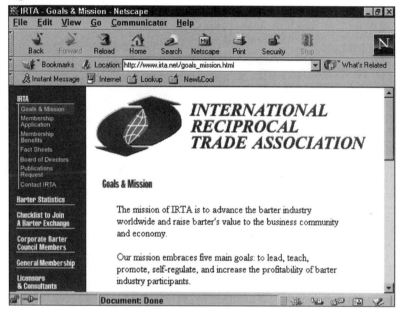

Table 7-4:   Online Barter Sites

Barter	Site URL
Art of Barter	www.barter1.com.
Barter Advantage	www.barteradv.com
Barter Business Network	www.bbnetwork.com
Barter Buys Online	www.barterbuys.com
BarterOne	www.barterone.com
eBarter	www.ebarter.com
International Reciprocal Trade Association (IRTA)	www.irta.net
National Association of Trade Exchanges (NATE)	www.nate.org
Trade Depot	www.Tradedepot.com
VIP Barter	www.vipbarter.com

CHAPTER 8
TAKING DELIVERY

IN THIS CHAPTER

- Picking a shipper
- Rating the cost
- Confirming delivery schedules
- Tracking your shipment online
- Using electronic distribution

With very rare exception, everything ordered on the Internet has to be put on a truck or plane, and everyone from the post office to UPS is just thrilled about all the new business. These companies have become very Web-friendly, so you can take care of all your shipping needs from your computer, including comparing companies, methods, and rates, tracking shipments online, and making sure that your delivery schedule is met. You can also find out about electronic distribution.

Picking a Shipper

Some online stores, just like their bricks-and-mortar equivalents, only have one shipper that they deal with. For instance, the online store may only use the postal service or UPS, and you may not even be able to choose from among the delivery options those outfits offer. However, with most large shopping sites, you get to pick both which company carries your package as well as whether the package is sent by air or ground.

Researching various shipping companies

Before you get heavily into shopping online, getting familiar with the major shipping companies is a good idea. Don't wait until you're already at the point of filling out an online order form before you confront the question. See Chapter 6 for more on filling out online order forms.

Table 8-1 shows the URLs of several major shipping companies, and Figure 8-1 shows you the Federal Express Web site.

Figure 8-1: The Federal Express Home page.

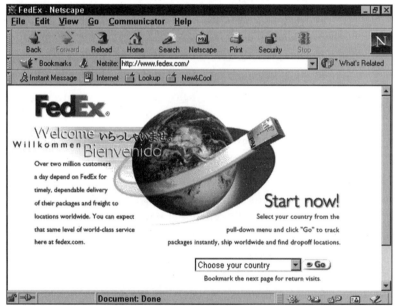

In addition to the shipping companies themselves, you can also deal with SmartShip (www.smartship.com/main.html). This site used to offer only price comparisons on the various shippers, but you can now use it to handle your shipping within the 50 United States. You just fill out the information online and they take care of arranging pickup and delivery with the service of your choice.

Table 8-1: Major Shipping Companies

Company	Home Page
Airborne Express	www.airborne-express.com
DHL	www.dhl.com
Federal Express	www.fedex.com
United Parcel Service	www.ups.com
U.S. Post Office	www.usps.gov

Comparing shipping rates

How much you pay for shipping depends on a number of factors, like:

- The distance the package is travelling.

- The type of packaging (such as tube, box, envelope, and so on).

- The dimensions and weight of the package.

- How quickly you want the package delivered.

Of these factors, the most important and personal is how fast you want it. If you *need* that new mystery novel as desperately (and quickly) as you need a replacement part for your dead computer, then you need to know the applicable rates, as well as how much they can vary from shipper to shipper. Table 8-2 shows the costs and delivery times for a hypothetical five-pound package sent from New York to Miami using a variety of shipping companies and methods.

Table 8-2: Shipping Price Comparisons

Shipping Method	Cost	Delivery Time
Federal Express Priority Overnight	$33.00	10:30 a.m. next day
Federal Express Standard Overnight	$28.25	3:00 p.m. next day

Shipping Method	Cost	Delivery Time
FedEx 2 day delivery	$14.50	4:30 p.m. in 2 days
Federal Express Express Saver	$13.45	4:30 p.m. in 3 days
UPS Next Day Air Early A.M	$54.75	8:30 a.m. next day
UPS Next Day Air	$29.75	10:30 a.m. next day
UPS Next Day Air Saver	$25.75	End of next day
UPS 2nd Day Air	$13.25	End of 2nd day
UPS 3 Day Select	$10.40	End of 3rd day
UPS Ground	$5.58	Around 3 days
USPS Express Mail	$24.00	Next day
USPS Priority Mail	$6.50	2 days
USPS Parcel Post	$6.45	4 days

Remember

If you order an item that's shipped on a Friday for Monday delivery, you may want to take a chance on using two-day delivery instead of overnight and save a little money in the process. Your item is in transit over the weekend, so you have a pretty good chance that your two-day delivery will come in on Monday, anyway

Knowing your other costs

If you're shopping the Web because of its ease and simplicity, or for the wide variety of products you can find, or for any of a thousand other reasons, then you're probably going to be pretty happy about what you purchase and what you pay for it. But if you're just looking for savings, you may be in for a bit of a shock. Regardless of how much or how little a product costs you, you can suddenly find yourself paying a lot more because of the extra costs, which include the following:

- **Handling:** While shipping costs are pretty cut-and-dry (see "Comparing shipping rates," in this chapter), *handling costs* are looser. A handling cost is the additional expense to the seller of paying an employee to get the product off the shelf, pack your purchase into a box, fill out the shipping manifest, and hand the package to the delivery service.

  Most handling fees are around $3.95, but sometimes they are higher. If you think you're being overcharged for a handling fee, ask the merchant to justify the cost before you finish filling out the online order form.

- **Sales Tax:** If you're purchasing an item from a merchant who is in your state, you probably have to pay sales tax. You don't pay sales tax if you're ordering an item across state lines or from a foreign country. If you order from a company with a presence in your state you may still get stuck paying sales tax.

- **Shipping Insurance:** Most shipments have some kind of insurance coverage included in the shipping cost, but you may want to add extra insurance for expensive items. You pay the extra cost.

Make sure that you know how much insurance there is on an item when you order it.

Table 8-3 shows you how to assess the extra costs for a five-pound item sent two-day delivery by Federal Express from New York to Miami. Just for fun, we added Florida's state tax into the mix to show you how the overall price can be affected.

Table 8-3:   How Extra Costs Affect Your Total Purchase

Seller's Price	Shipper's Price	Handling	6.5% Sales Tax	Final Total
$15	14.50	$4	$0.98	$34.48
$30	$14.50	$7	$1.95	$53.45

If you're shopping for a bargain, getting a book at $3.00 off the list price may not be so great if you have to pay $7.00 for shipping and handling.

Knowing When Your Package Should Arrive

Before you finish placing an order, you need to know just how long a seller expects getting the item from the warehouse to the shipping company. You also need to know how to track your package while it's en route to you. Finally, you should know the laws that spell out the seller's shipping responsibilities.

When you place an order, make sure you ask:

- Is the item you're ordering actually in stock?

- If not, how long will it be on back order?

Tracking your shipment online

Every major shipping company has an online tracking system. All you have to do is to log on to a shipper's Web site and click the link that says something like `track your package`. From there, just enter the tracking number for your order and you can find out in real time just exactly where the package is and where it's been. Figure 8-2 shows UPS's tracking page.

Knowing a seller's shipping responsibilities

A federal law covers delivery time limits for items you order on the Internet. The law is called the Mail or Telephone Order Merchandise Rule, and you can find it at

```
www.ftc.gov/bcp/conline/pubs/buspubs/
mailordr/mailrule.htm.
```

Companies have different requirements under the law, such as:

■ If a company specifies a shipping timeline, such as a statement on its online order form that says allow three to four weeks for delivery, then the company is required to meet its deadline.

■ If a company doesn't specify a delivery time, then the company automatically has 30 days from the day you place your order to ship the product.

■ If a company can't meet its shipping schedule, then it is required to notify you of the delay and offer you the option to cancel or maintain your order.

Warning

If a company attempts to contact you to give you the option of backing out of your order and receives no response, the company can (and probably will) leave the order standing.

Figure 8-2: The UPS tracking system.

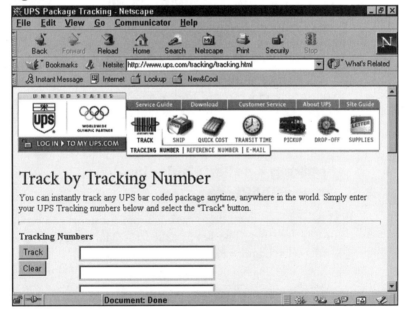

If a merchant doesn't send an item to you within the time-frame required by law, or worse yet, if the package never arrives, see Chapter 9 for details on handling the situation.

Making Sure You Get the Item

If you work a 9-to-5 job, what good is it to get a package delivered to your door at 10 in the morning? Here are some suggestions to help ensure you receive the item you order:

■ If you're never at home during business hours, have the package delivered to your place of business, but first make sure you know your company's policy on receiving personal packages during work time.

■ If you're not home the first time an attempt is made to deliver your item and the delivery person leaves you a note, sign the note and hang it back on your door. The next day the delivery person will leave your package.

■ If the delivery company has a warehouse near you, you can usually take the release form in and pick up the package a few hours after delivery was attempted.

■ If you receive deliveries regularly, you can arrange a *permanent release* with the delivery company so that you don't ever have to sign a note or release ever again, and the company can always leave packages for you without any hassle. Call the phone number on the delivery note and ask about this option.

■ If you know you won't be home when the package arrives, leave a note taped to your door that authorizes the delivery person to leave the package on your doorstep or with a neighbor. Your signature and printed name and address make the note as official as the delivery company's release form.

Using Electronic Distribution

If you're ordering something that can be sent over the Internet, then you can take advantage of electronic distribution. Basically, that means you can download the product using your web browser or have the product sent to you as an e-mail attachment. This is only useful for items such as

- Books (those that are available in electronic form)
- Newsletters
- Reports
- Software

The advantage to electronically receiving products from the Internet is that you don't even have to wait for delivery — although the download time for a major program can take hours over a slow modem connection.

Small software firms have long used *electronic software distribution,* or ESD, to avoid having to deal with packaging and shipping costs, and now major software publishers have jumped on the bandwagon. Figure 8-3 shows the Macromedia Web site, where you can purchase and download commercial programs such as Fireworks and Dreamweaver.

If you order a software program online, you often get some kind of extra benefit (like extra clip art or utility programs) if you have it shipped.

Figure 8-3:   You can download some purchases electronically.

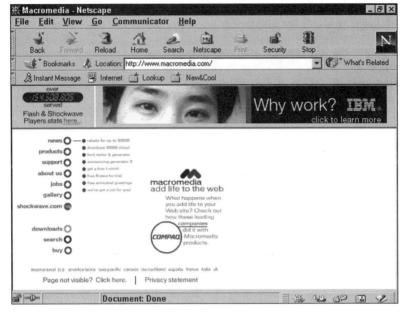

CHAPTER 9

HANDLING TRANSACTION PROBLEMS

IN THIS CHAPTER

- Working with the merchant
- Documenting your claim
- Complaining to credit card companies
- Getting the government involved

Sooner or later, somewhere along the line, you're going to run into a problem. Perhaps a product isn't quite what you thought it was, or a company fails to honor its stated return policy. Just as in the real world, disputes occasionally arise in cyberspace.

In this chapter, you can learn how to document your dealings and use simple and gentle approaches for working with a merchant. We also show you how to pursue more drastic measures, if necessary, such as filing claims with creditors and government agencies.

Keeping Records

Unfortunately, you never know when you may have a problem come up, so we recommend that you hang on to all of your documentation of a transaction just in case. The more organized you are, the better your chances of resolving a transaction-related problem in your favor. You've got to prepare the same kind of evidence that you'd present to a judge, anyway. Make sure you've got all the paperwork that's involved in the transaction and follow these rules and prepare for a possible problem from the word go:

- **Trace your steps.** Make a printout of every Web page involved in every step of the process, including completed online order form.

- **Save all e-mail correspondence,** including order confirmations.

- **Keep everything together and keep it safe.** Put all the printed materials into a folder and set the folder aside.

Working with the Merchant

Most of the time, disputes can be settled by talking to a merchant. This advice may sound naïve, good merchants are fully aware of two important factors in business:

- Merchants depend on their living on keeping your business.

- If you're unhappy with a merchant, you will tell your friends.

This means that many merchants are usually eager to avoid or solve any legitimate problem with the least amount of fuss.

Picking your battles: Legitimate problems

The key word if disputing a transaction is *legitimate.* If you're being unreasonable, or if a merchant doesn't think that you have a real basis for your complaint, then even the most accommodating people will probably balk at refunding your money or accepting a return. Some typical legitimate problems that you should discuss with a merchant include:

- A product doesn't do what it was supposed to do, such as software that doesn't work on the operating system for which it was advertised.

- You receive the wrong product, such as a shirt that isn't the color ordered.

- The product is *D.O.A.,* or in unworkable condition.

- The price on the invoice is higher than you expected.

Resolving a problem professionally

If you have a legitimate problem with a product that you've purchased online, do the following to resolve the issue directly with the merchant:

1. Calm down. If you're mad, take a breather. You accomplish nothing if you come across as aggressive.

2. Assemble and read through the documentation you have on the transaction. Read the fine print to see if you've made an error or interpreted information incorrectly.

3. Come up with a plan for handling the problem. For example, if you've purchased, opened, and installed software that doesn't work properly, but the company's return policy clearly states that it will not give refunds on opened software, then focus your plan around asking for replacement software instead.

4. Contact the company's customer service department to tell the company's representative the nature of the problem, and what you'd like done to fix the problem. Then offer a tentative timeline for resolving the problem.

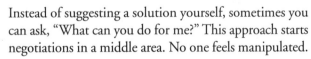

Instead of suggesting a solution yourself, sometimes you can ask, "What can you do for me?" This approach starts negotiations in a middle area. No one feels manipulated.

5. Write down everything said in the call, including the number you call, the date and time of the call, and the name of the person to whom you spoke.

When taking notes on conversations, do your best to fully characterize the other person's attitude as well as his or her words. Whether the person you're dealing with is conciliatory or nasty to you when you try to solve a problem can make a big difference down the road.

6. Do not hang up until you have found a resolution, even if that resolution is to a smaller problem. (For example, you're told that before you can get a refund for your broken software, someone in the company's technical support department needs to verify that a program is indeed defective.)

As a last ditch trick, if you don't have possession of the item — if you returned it to the merchant — then you don't owe for it.

Using Your Credit Card Company as a Resource

We hope you never need to use the information in this section, but if you made an online purchase with a credit card, you have some legal protections offered by your credit card company.

Don't assume that your creditor is on your side. You may lose a dispute with a credit card company if you don't have a well-documented case.

If all a credit card company has in a dispute is your word against a merchant's word, you probably won't be successful unless the credit card company has a lot of complaints against that merchant, or your case represents a really obvious case of fraud.

Understanding the FCBA

Before you file a claim with your credit card company, you need to know about the *Fair Credit Billing Act* (Title 15, Section 1666 of the U.S. Code), or FCBA for short. FCBA gives you certain rights, including the following, if you dispute a credit card charge:

■ You don't have to pay the amount in dispute on your bill while the transaction is in dispute.

■ Your credit rating cannot be trashed over a credit company or merchant's mistake.

■ The creditor has certain actions it must take after you make a claim and, if the creditor doesn't take these steps, it may end up losing money.

Filing a claim

Maintaining your paper trail is even more important if you decide to file a claim with a creditor. You should

■ **Always** file credit card claims in writing.

■ **Always** send the claim using the U.S. Postal Service's certified mail, and request to have a return receipt so that you know when your claim is received by the creditor.

■ **Never** call the creditor's 800 number instead of writing a letter.

■ **Never** send the creditor your claim as an e-mail message.

Tip

The date and time your claim is received by the creditor is a critical part of enforcing your rights under the FCBA.

You should send your claim in the form of a letter that *arrives* to the creditor no longer than 60 days after the creditor *sent* the bill to you. In practical terms, that means you really only have about 50 days to file your claim from the day you receive the bill.

Your letter to the credit card company must include the following:

- Your name and account number
- The amount of the disputed charge
- The nature of the error or dispute

Although not required by law, you should also include the following:

- The name of the person or company from whom you bought the item in question.
- The date you made the purchase.
- The date the purchase was posted to your account.
- The reference number on your bill for that purchase.
- Your address and your daytime and evening telephone numbers.
- A photocopy of the statement with the disputed purchase circled.
- Supporting documentation, such as receipts, copies of return shipping air bills, a copy of the merchant's return policy. Do not send originals.

As soon as the credit card company gets your claim letter, it must do the following:

- Respond in writing within 30 days of the date your letter was received. The response must acknowledge that you have filed a claim under the Fair Credit Billing Act.
- Conduct an investigation into your claim.
- Either resolve the problem in your favor or send you a letter within two billing cycles (or 90 days) explaining why your claim has been denied.

During the time the dispute is under investigation, you don't have to pay the amount (including applicable finance charges) of your credit card statement that is in dispute. If the investigation determines that you must pay for the item, however, you must also pay any finance charges that accrued.

Credit card companies can't so much as *threaten* to take any action to collect the amount that's in dispute while an investigation is going on without breaking the law. The transaction may still legally appear on your monthly statement, however.

Most credit card companies offer two addresses for sending correspondence. If you don't send your letter to the right address, the creditor isn't required to obey the law. Use the address that appears under a heading that reads something like `If you find an error or have a question about your bill.`

If your credit card company has treated you unfairly, you can file a claim with the Federal Trade Commission (see "Getting the Government Involved" later in this chapter).

Preventing Other Payment Losses

If you purchase an item using another payment method, such as a debit card, check, or cash, you don't have the same protection as you do with a credit card. However, you're still not totally defenseless, especially if you use a debit card. The *Electronic Fund Transfer Act* (EFTA), while not as useful as the FCBA, still gives you some coverage.

Technically, you can stop payment on a check if you don't receive the item, but few companies ship items until the check clears. If you pay for a product with cash or a check, you're just plain out of luck if the transaction goes bad — unless you want to go to court.

Under the EFTA, banks are required to respond to claims within 10 days. Here are some of the other aspects of the law:

- You can initially notify your bank of a billing error over the phone, you may be required to confirm the notification in writing.

- Banks can arbitrarily decide to take 45 days (and up to 90 days under some circumstances) instead of 10 days to investigate, but a bank has to credit your debit account with the amount of the disputed charge.

- The EFTA allows banks to withhold crediting your account for up to $50 of the disputed amount. For instance, if your account is fairly new, a bank can balk.

Seek an attorney's advice if you have any problems with a debit card transaction. Because each debit card issuer can set its own rules, the absolute least you should do is make sure that you know what your bank expects of you and what it will do for you if you suspect there is a problem with your account.

Getting the Government Involved

If you've really been ripped off — not just a basic dispute over minor differences, but an out-and-out criminal situation — then you may want to call the authorities. In the case of Internet fraud, the proper authorities are the *Federal Trade Commission* (FTC), the United States Postal Service, or your state government.

- The *Federal Trade Commission* (FTC) is the major national agency responsible for regulating commercial operations. The FTC also provides the main federal links page to federal agencies that deal with a variety of problems, called the Consumer Gateway, at `www.con-sumer.gov`.

- The FTC has a branch called the *Bureau of Consumer Protection* (BCP), which provides consumers with information and has a complaint form so that you can report online and bricks-and-mortar companies that have allegedly committed fraud. You can check out the BCP at `www.ftc.gov/ftc/consumer.htm`. Use the BCP's claim form (`www.ftc.gov/ftc/complaint.htm`) to file a federal claim against a company.

- *United States Postal Inspection Service* (USPIS) investigates cases of fraud that involve the United States mail. Postal inspectors are federal law enforcement officers with plenty on their plate from insurance fraud to child pornography. To locate the nearest Postal Inspection Service office, go to `www.usps.gov/ncsc/locators/find-is.html` shown in Figure 9-1. The USPIS's URL is `www.usps.gov/websites/depart/inspect`.

Remember

  The post office cannot do anything about shipments that are sent UPS or Federal Express, or through another shipping agency.

- Your state government's *Consumer Protection Agency* can help you prosecute nefarious merchants. Find your state government's main Web site by using the following general Web address, replacing the **xx** with the two letter postal code for your state. If you're looking for the California State government site, type **ca** in place of **xx** (`www.state.xx.us`).

- Your state's *Attorney General* can also prosecute negligent and fraudulent merchants. Track down your Attorney General via the National Association of Attorneys General Web site: `www.naag.org` (see Figure 9-2).

Table 9-1 gives you information on each of these law enforcement agencies and what they can do for you. Don't forget that you can also report less-than-perfect (or downright criminal) merchants to the Better Business Bureau (see Chapter 2).

Figure 9-1: The Postal Inspection Service search form.

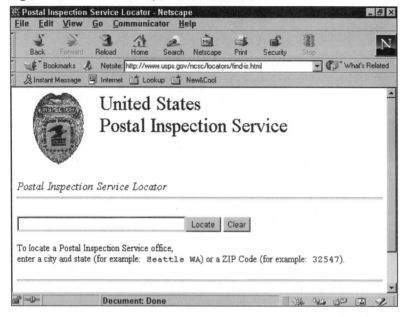

Figure 9-2: The Attorney General search form.

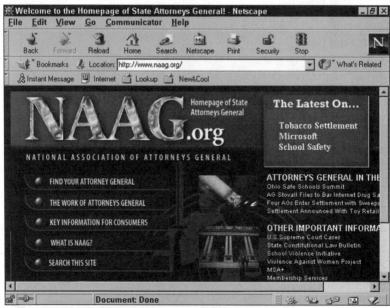

Table 9-1: Federal and State Law Enforcement Resources

Agency	Investigates	What It Does For You	Watch Out
Federal Trade Commission	Companies with a multiple allegations; questionable conduct in multiple companies	All consumers benefit from the FTC's successful prosecutions	Slow to catch up with Internet technology
Bureau of Consumer Protection	No one. This is the arm of the FTC that provides information	Use the BCP's information to keep safe; use its claim form to file complaints against retailers	May not pay much attention to a claim unless the allegations are part of a large-scale investigation
United States Postal Inspection Service	Suspects who use the U.S. mail to defraud consumers	The USPIS can prosecute if a suspect used the U.S. mail at some point during the commission of a crime	USPIS only stretches the law in significant situations and does not investigate petty problems
Your state's Consumer Protection Agency	Files lawsuits or brings charges against merchants who break state laws	Deals with individual cases and uses legal muscle on your behalf	May move slowly against merchants
Your state's Attorney General	Files lawsuits or brings charges against merchants who break state laws	Deals with individual cases and uses legal muscle on your behalf	Interested in high-profile cases

CLIFFSNOTES REVIEW

Use this CliffsNotes Review to practice what you've learned in this book and to build your confidence in doing the job right the first time. After you work through the review questions, the scenario questions, the visual test, and the fun and useful practice projects, you're well on your way to achieving your goal of shopping online like a pro.

Q&A

1. For the greatest legal protection, you should always pay with:
   a. A credit card.
   b. Electronic cash.
   c. A debit card.

2. The best source for information about a product is:
   a. The manufacturer.
   b. A current customer.
   c. A magazine ad.

3. The utility that tells you who owns a domain name is called:
   a. WhosThat.
   b. WhoIs.
   c. WhatsIt.

4. A trustmark is:
   a. An award for trustworthiness.
   b. Proof that a Web site operates a secure server.
   c. A symbol that a Web site abides by an association's standards.

5. Which shipping service can ship to a post office box?

    a. United Parcel Service.

    b. U.S. Postal Service.

    c. Federal Express.

6. ESD stands for _____.

7. The federal agency responsible for dealing with Internet fraud is:

    a. The FBI.

    b. The FCC.

    c. The FTC.

8. The part of an online order form where you enter your name is called:

    a. A drop-down list.

    b. A check box.

    c. A text box.

Answers: (1) a. (2) b. (3) b. (4) c. (5) b. (6) Electronic Software Distribution. (7) c. (8) c.

Scenario

1. You receive an e-mail message from a stranger offering you an incredible deal on a product that you're interested in buying. You should _____

_____.

2. You really want to buy a product from an online store, but the store's Web site doesn't have a secure server. You should _____

_____

_____.

3. A Web site asks you for personal information but doesn't have a posted privacy policy. You should_____

_____

_____.

4. You're expecting a package to arrive today, but it hasn't arrived yet. You should_____

_____

_____.

Answers: (1) Ignore the offer and delete the e-mail message. (2) Place the order by phone, fax, or snail mail instead. (3) Send the Webmaster an e-mail message asking what the Web site does with the personal information it's provided in questionnaires. (4) Use the tracking services of the shipper on their Web site to see where the package is. If the package doesn't arrive within a five days of its anticipated arrival-date, contact the seller to see what's going on.

Consider This

- Did you know that many shopping Web sites have newsletters that you can receive by e-mail? If you subscribe to one of these newsletters, you can get news on the site's latest new products as they come in. But make sure you check out the Web site's privacy policy before you subscribe to its newsletter, or you may end up getting lots of junk mail if they sell your name and e-mail address to other companies.

- Did you know that you can often get a lower price for an item than the listed one? If you can find more than one Web site that is selling a product, compare the prices. Maybe one site has a lower price, but another has better service. If you'd rather buy the item from the site with the higher price (but the better service), ask if the merchant can meet or beat its competitors' lower price. Most merchants are sensitive to being the low price leader and will quickly agree.

Practice Project

Pick an item you're interested in purchasing online and then track it down using the following Internet resources:

1. Go to an online auction house and check to see if the product is currently available for bidding. Then check the high bids on the item, as well as if the product comes with a warranty. See Chapter 7 for more information.

2. Try out a few of the price comparison Web sites to find out the current retail price for the product. See Chapter 3 for more information.

   Go to the online version of a bricks-and-mortar store that sells the product and compare the online store's product selection, price, and service with its physical store counterpart. See Chapter 1 for more information.

CLIFFSNOTES RESOURCE CENTER

The learning doesn't need to stop here. CliffsNotes Resource Center shows you the best of the best — links to the best information in print and online about shopping online. Look for all the terrific resources at your favorite bookstore or local library and on the Internet. When you're online, make your first stop www.cliffsnotes.com, where you can find more incredibly useful information about shopping online safely.

Books

This CliffsNotes book is one of many great books about the Internet published by IDG Books Worldwide, Inc. So if you want some great next-step books, check out some of these other publications:

Buying Online For Dummies, by Joseph Lowery, tips you to the best virtual stores and the right products at the right prices, all from the comfort of your home or office computer. You'll find helpful advice to make secure transactions over the Net, buy and sell through online classified ads, and set up your own Internet connection optimized for online shopping. Be sure to check out this book's 70+ pages of great online outlets — from travel services to books and music — and the book's bonus CD-ROM, which includes current versions of both Netscape and Microsoft web browsers as well as other cool shareware and freeware programs to make your online shopping experience fun, safe, and hassle-free. IDG Books Worldwide, $24.99

Banking Online For Dummies, by Paul A. Murphy. Standing in long lines at the bank is a thing of the past. Discover ways to save yourself time and money by banking online. Even if you've never logged on to the World Wide Web before, Banking Online For Dummies brings you all the information and software you need to get started right away in doing all your banking online — and taking real control of your money. Banking Online For Dummies guides you safely through the mysteries of online banking, from banking basics to advanced advice on finding, using, and understanding the latest e-commerce and banking news online. Discover the ease of managing all your money with several popular financial software packages — including Managing Your Money, QuickBooks and QuickBooks Pro, Microsoft Money, and AOL BankNOW — as you master the skills of transferring funds, reviewing your accounts online, paying bills, and more. Plus, the book comes with a bonus CD-ROM that includes Netscape Navigator and Internet Explorer web browsers, trial versions of QuickBooks and QuickBooks Pro, and direct links to the entire universe of online resources listed in the book. IDG Books Worldwide, $24.99.

You can easily find books published by IDG Books Worldwide, Inc., in your favorite bookstores, at the library, on the Internet, and at a store near you. We also have three Web sites that you can use to read about all the books we publish:

    www.dummies.com

    www.idgbooks.com

    www.cliffsnotes.com

Internet

Check out these Web sites for more information about the Internet:

www.shoplet.com/index.html takes you to the *Internet Shopping Outlet*, where you can pick from over 4,000,000 products, including books and computer equipment.

`www.helpschildren.com` is the location of *Online Shopping Helps Children's Hospital*, which is exactly what it sounds like. Half of the commissions earned by this shopping mall site from your purchases are donated to help sick children.

`www.familyshopper.com` leads to *Family Shopper*, where you can buy books, games, music, software, toys, and videos.

`www.shoppingmallsdirectory.com` is the URL for *The Internet Shopping Malls Directory*, a Web site that gives you tons of links to all kinds of shopping experiences.

`www.shopunet.com/index.htm` takes you to the *Shopunet Shopping Directory and Buying Guide*, where you can do price comparisons, read up on product reviews, and check out their ratings of online stores.

`www.alltherightgifts.com` is the location for *All the Right Gifts*, a shopping site with links for everything you can think of to buy online — from health food to cars.

`www.freeshop.com` leads to *FreeShop*, where you can sift through lots of offers for free samples, coupons, trial subscriptions, and the like.

`www.shopguide.co.uk` takes you to *ShopGuide*, which rates and reviews hundreds of online stores and helps you to find the best price for a product, too.

`webshoppingzone.com` is the URL for the *Web Shopping Zone*, an online mall with eight different "floors."

`shopweb.net` is *Shopweb*, a links page for dozens of online stores from sporting goods to groceries.

`mall.weborbiter.com` leads to *Web Orbiter! — Online Shopping Index*, with links to more stores than you could wander through in a week.

`www.webpagesnow.com` is the location of *Web Pages Now: Your Online Shopping Guide*, which reviews online stores for you.

Next time you're on the Internet, don't forget to drop by `www.cliffsnotes.com`. We created an online Resource Center that you can use today, tomorrow, and beyond.

Send Us Your Favorite Tips

In your quest for knowledge, have you ever experienced that sublime moment when you figure out a trick that saves time or trouble? Perhaps you realized you were taking ten steps to accomplish something that could take two. Or you found a little-known workaround that achieved great results. If you've discovered a useful tip that helped you browse the Internet more effectively, and you'd like to share it, the CliffsNotes staff would love to hear from you. Go to our Web site at `www.cliffsnotes.com` and look for the Talk to Us button. If we select your tip, we may publish it as part of *CliffsNotes Daily*, our exciting, free e-mail newsletter. To find out more, or to subscribe to the newsletter, go to `www.cliffsnotes.com` on the Web.

INDEX

CliffsNotes™

Your shortcut to success™ for over 40 years

Computers and Software
Confused by computers? Struggling with software? Let *CliffsNotes* get you up to speed on the fundamentals — quickly and easily. Titles include:

Balancing Your Checkbook with Quicken®
Buying Your First PC
Creating a Dynamite PowerPoint® 2000 Presentation
Making Windows® 98 Work for You
Setting up a Windows® 98 Home Network
Upgrading and Repairing Your PC
Using Your First PC
Using Your First iMac™
Writing Your First Computer Program

The Internet
Intrigued by the Internet? Puzzled about life online?
Let *CliffsNotes* show you how to get started with e-mail, Web surfing, and more. Titles include:

Buying and Selling on eBay®
Creating Web Pages with HTML
Creating Your First Web Page
Exploring the Internet with Yahoo!®
Finding a Job on the Web
Getting on the Internet
Going Online with AOL®
Shopping Online Safely